NOTHING SHALL BY ANY MEANS HURT YOU

KNOWING THE SECRETS OF DARKNESS AND HOW TO OVERCOME THEM

AYODEJI DAVID OLUSANMI

Nothing Shall By Any Means Hurt You
by Ayodeji David Olusanmi

Interior design and editing by SPBookdesign

ISBN: 978-1-5136-2029-9

Contact Copyright Holder at

Ayodeji D. Olusanmi
Baruch Publishing
152 Oval Road North
Dagenham, Essex
RM10 9EH
England
a.ilesanmi85@yahoo.co.uk

Behold, I give unto you power to tread on serpents and scorpions, and over all the power of the enemy: and
NOTHING SHALL BY ANY MEANS HURT YOU.
LUKE 10:19

DEDICATION

I DEDICATE THIS BOOK TO MY WIFE – MARGARET OLUWA-SEUN OLUSANMI – WHO HAS BEEN A TREMENDOUS HELPER TO MY LIFE AND MINISTRY. INDEED, A HELPER SUITABLE FOR ME!

APPRECIATION

We are to give honour to whom it is due. I would like to honour Dr Daniel K. Olukoya, the General Overseer of Mountain of Fire and Miracles Ministries Worldwide for all he has done and is doing for me. Daddy, your impact in my life can not be quantified. My wife and I love you. I thank God for giving me a place to serve in MFM. It is an honour to partake of your grace Sir.

I would also like to honour Rev & Rev (Mrs) Olusola Areogun, the General Overseer of Life Oasis International Church (The Dream Centre). Daddy, Mummy, my wife and I are grateful for the words you have sown in our lives over the years that we have followed your ministry. My wife and I appreciate the wisdom that comes to us from you anytime we are privileged to meet with you. We treasure those moments.

I would like to honour Pastor (Mrs) Tinu Olajide as well, Assistant Regional Overseer, Mountain of Fire and Miracle Ministries, Sweden & Finland. Firstly, for your constant spiritual/moral input and guidance into the life of my wife and I. Secondly, for taking time out to help edit, correct and proofread the manuscripts. Your input is appreciated.

Finally, I also honour those who have been a blessing to me over the years. God will reward your labour of love.

Amen

CONTENTS

INTRODUCTION

THE DEVIL IS an expert in hurting people, that is what he loves to do – to cause pain to mankind. This gives him joy and fulfilment.

The bible says, "And we know that we are of God, and ***the whole world lieth in wickedness***" 1John 5:19

We know that we are children of God and ***that all the rest of the world around us is under Satan's power and control*** (TLB)

We know [for a fact] that we are of God, and ***the whole world [around us] lies in the power of the evil one [opposing God and His precepts]***. (AMP)

Did you notice that it says **THE WHOLE WORLD LIETH IN WICKEDNESS...THE REST OF THE WORLD AROUND US IS UNDER SATAN'S POWER AND CONTROL.**

That is a big and bold statement. It didn't say some part of the world is under the control of Satan. It says the WHOLE WORLD! Some people think wickedness is only in Africa. Friends, wickedness is everywhere. It is in Asia, America, and Europe. It is everywhere!

As long as you are in the world, the bible says there is wickedness around you. Though you are of God, the man next to you may be of the Devil and that is wickedness before you.

It is therefore imperative that we know how this wickedness works in hurting people so we can be better equipped in fighting it. In life, you must not only know yourself, you must also know the enemy, it's weaknesses and strengths. The Olympic medallists study their rival keenly, to know all there is to know about the person. This is what you have in every game of sports – knowing the opponents well. Victory is impossible without the adequate knowledge of your rival.

> "Lest Satan should get an advantage of us: **for we are not ignorant of his devices**" 2Cor 2:11.

Paul says here that the Devil will get an advantage (he will have an upper hand or he will be better positioned) if we don't know his devices. The word translated **"DEVICES"** here is from the Greek word **"NOEMA"**. It means a mental perception, thought, an evil purpose, that which thinks, the mind. These are the things we must know.

We must know the plans, mind and purpose of the enemy. We must know how he thinks and operates. His tricks must not be strange to us. God is faithful, he shows us some of these things in whatever way or manner he deems fit.

We can study the tricks the enemy has used before because it's likely he will repeat them. The device he used for Judas was money. He used women for Samson – Delilah to be specific and Eve's bait was fruit (a sign of desire to be independent).

The equation is like this:

Judas = Money

Samson = Women (Delilah)

Eve = Fruit

You =?

One thing that confronted me whilst writing this introduction is the major means through which the enemy/devil hurts people is through the individual's weaknesses.

Seeing this, we must give careful attention to our weaknesses and ensure that by the help of the Holy Spirit, we crucify the flesh, it affections and lusts (See Gal 5:24).

The weakness you permit and excuse today will destroy you tomorrow. Kill it before it kills you.

As I bring this introduction to a close, in the following chapters we shall be looking at what it means to be hurt. We shall look at the various channels through which the enemy hurts people –the weapons the enemy deploys against people.

We will also look at some of the reasons why and when the enemy hurt people.

Finally, we shall see the fighting strategy we can use against the evil plans of the enemy. Here we will see practical steps to be taken to always be ahead of the enemy.

I trust the Lord that He will open your understanding as you read. I pray that light will break out for you and you will not enter the trap of the evil one.

Behold, I give unto you power to tread on serpents and scorpions, and over all the power of the enemy: and **nothing shall by any means hurt you.**
Luke 10:19

Chapter One

WHAT IT MEANS TO BE HURT

"He sent a man before them, even Joseph, who was sold for a servant: **WHOSE FEET THEY HURT WITH FETTERS: HE WAS LAID IN IRON**: *Until the time that his word came: the word of the Lord tried him. The king sent and loosed him; even the ruler of the people, and let him go free."*
Ps 105:17-20

IT IS OBVIOUS that from the Psalmist account of what happened to Joseph, beginning from how God called for a famine in Egypt and how he was sent to the same Egypt to preserve life, Joseph had gone through a measure of hurt. The bible is very detailed in the transfer of Joseph from his place of birth to the land of slavery – Egypt. Did you notice that the bible says of Joseph that his, "…FEET THEY HURT WITH FETTERS: HE WAS LAID IN IRON…"?

That shows the level of discomfort he suffered. Whilst he was being transported to Egypt, both his hands and feet were in chains. To hurt is to have limited freedom.

During the slavery era, when slaves were sold, they were often loaded in ships with hands and feet bound. That was exactly what Joseph experienced. A 1997 film *Roots* paints a good picture.

To hurt is to damage something. Joseph's brother damaged his clothing; they did more than just cloth damage though. They also damaged his person. You might not understand until you are betrayed by your own brothers who are meant to care and defend you. As brothers, we should have each other's back, not plan to hurt each other. Sometimes in life, it is those who should love and comfort us that are orchestrating our downfall. But it is written, "...NOTHING SHALL BY ANY MEANS HURT US".

Joseph was separated from the love of a father and sold into hostility.

To hurt is to do wrong against. It means to harm, act unjustly against, to injure both physically and spiritually. Joseph in every sense experienced this.

PAUL AND SILAS WERE HURT

"And the multitude rose up together against them: and the magistrates rent off their clothes, and commanded to beat them. ***And when they had laid many stripes upon them****, they cast them into prison, charging the jailor to keep them safely: Who, having received such a charge, thrust them into the inner prison, and made their feet fast in the stocks....And he took them the same hour of the night, and* ***washed their stripes****; and was baptized, he and all his, straightway"* **ACTS 16:22-24 &33**

Paul had just cast out a Devil – spirit of Python (Divination) – from a girl who had brought much gain to her owners. The owners were mad because their business had suffered a major setback. They stirred up the people against Paul and Silas until they were not only imprisoned, they were physically hurt. The bible says the people, "*.....laid many stripes upon them, they cast them into prison, charging the jailor to keep them safely...*"

The Apostles were physically beaten. Later, when they were released, the bible shows the level of care they received, "*...And he took them the same hour of the night, and WASHED THEIR STRIPES...*"

Washing their stripes means the keeper of the prison nursed their wounds. He applied some form of medication to reduce the pain. There are some physical discomforts people go through that are manifestations of the power of darkness. Never be naïve. Don't ever take anything for granted.

Paul had done deliverance by casting out a spirit, and that action met with a counter attack.

JESUS DEALT WITH TWO DEMONS THAT BROUGHT HURT ON THE VICTIM

MAD MAN OF GADARENE – **Mark 5:1-6**

"And they came over unto the other side of the sea, into the country of the Gadarenes. And when he was come out of the ship, immediately there met him out of the tombs a man with an unclean spirit, Who had his dwelling among the tombs; and no man could bind him, no, not with chains: Because that he had been often bound with fetters and chains, and the chains had been plucked asunder by him, and the fetters broken in pieces: neither could any man tame him. AND ALWAYS, ***NIGHT AND DAY, HE WAS IN THE MOUNTAINS, AND IN THE TOMBS, CRYING, AND CUTTING HIMSELF WITH STONES.*** *But when he saw Jesus afar off, he ran and worshipped him."*

As Jesus went about his evangelistic/outreach mission he met different people, situations and circumstances. We will look at two separate events.

Firstly, when he got to the place called Gadarene, he met a man in whom was an unclean spirit. The unclean spirit did something to that man, "*...had his dwelling among the tombs; and no man could bind him, no, not with chains...*"

You see, because there was a spirit in this man he loved to sleep in the cemetery. Whenever a strange spirit is at work in a man he will do strange things! Who in his or her right mind sleeps in a cemetery? No one!

The unclean spirit also made him to, "*...ALWAYS,* ***NIGHT AND***

***DAY, HE WAS IN THE MOUNTAINS, AND IN THE TOMBS,* CRYING, *AND* CUTTING HIMSELF WITH STONES....”**

This man was continually hurting himself. The spirit made him cry night and day and he would also CUT HIMSELF WITH STONES. So, he had what we call self-inflicted pains. He had no awareness of what was happening. His natural sense and ability to feel pain had been taking over by the unclean spirit.

The devil was hurting this man mentally, physically and spiritually.

A BOY WITH A DUMB AND DEAF SPIRIT – **Mark 9: 17-22**

“And one of the multitude answered and said, Master, I have brought unto thee my son, which hath a dumb spirit; And wheresoever he taketh him, ***HE TEARETH HIM: AND HE FOAMETH, AND GNASHETH WITH HIS TEETH, AND PINETH AWAY****: and I spake to thy disciples that they should cast him out; and they could not. He answereth him, and saith, O faithless generation, how long shall I be with you? how long shall I suffer you? bring him unto me. And they brought him unto him: and when he saw him, straightway* ***the spirit tare him; and he fell on the ground, and wallowed foaming.*** *And he asked his father, How long is it ago since this came unto him? And he said, Of a child. And* ***ofttimes it hath cast him into the fire, and into the waters, to destroy him****: but if thou canst do any thing, have compassion on us, and help us.”*

This was a situation Jesus had to confront because the Apostles could not help the boy in whom there was a spirit. Jesus knew it wasn’t an operation of a dumb spirit, the same spirit also made him deaf. If there is anything you should know about demons and spirits is that they don’t operate alone. They have a gang.

There is what is called GANG DEMONS. For example, if you see a demon of lust in a person, the next demon you will find is the demon of immorality manifesting in sexual perversion – adultery, fornication, masturbation and other sexual lust.

In the case of this boy, there was a spirit of dumbness and Jesus discerned a spirit of deafness. Note that though these are spirit of dumbness and deafness, the spirit in themselves are neither deaf nor dumb though that is their outworking in the life of the victim. So, you can address them in the name of Jesus, they will hear you and leave.

When Jesus addressed the spirit see what happened, "*And they brought him (The boy) unto him (Jesus): and when he (The spirit in the boy) saw him (Jesus),* ***straightway the spirit tare him****; and he fell on the ground, and* ***wallowed foaming.***"

Jesus asked the father, "*How long is it ago since this came unto him...*" He replied with something strange, "*.And he said, Of a child. And ofttimes It (****The Demon****) hath cast him into the fire, and into the waters, (****with the sole reason****) to destroy (****hurt****) him*".

Did you notice that the unclean spirit – demon – knew exactly what he wanted to achieve with the boy – to destroy or hurt him. That was why he would push him into the FIRE and WATER. If the fire wouldn't burn him the water would drown him.

Having seen what it means to be hurt, we will go on to the next chapter where we will see some of the methods – weapons – the enemy uses to hurt people.

Behold, I give unto you power to tread on serpents and scorpions, and over all the power of the enemy: and **nothing shall by any means hurt you.**
Luke 10:19

Chapter Two

WEAPONS THE ENEMY USES TO HURT PEOPLE

"Lest Satan should get an advantage of us: FOR WE ARE NOT IGNORANT OF ***HIS DEVICES****".*
2COR 2:11

*"**NO WEAPON THAT IS FORMED AGAINST THEE SHALL PROSPER**; and every tongue that shall rise against thee in judgment thou shalt condemn. This is the heritage of the servants of the Lord, and their righteousness is of me, saith the Lord."*
IS 54:17

"Behold, I give unto you power to tread on serpents and scorpions, and over all the power of the enemy: and NOTHING SHALL BY ***ANY MEANS*** *HURT YOU."*
Luke 10:19

The enemy can and has the power to hurt people, in fact he can kill. Jesus said, "*. . . . fear not them which kill the body. . . .*" Mat 10:28. Jesus clearly states that there are some categories of people who can KILL THE BODY. They have enough demonic power to hurt. It is foolishness for a believer to think that these sets of people do not exist. To be naïve on the battle ground is to be captured by the enemy.

There are weapons and devices the enemy deploy against individuals to hurt them. What we want to do is to look at some of these weapons and see how they work. This list is not exhaustive.

One thing we know is that in every battle, there are weapons that both sides use. What I know certainly is that the Christian man is not defenceless; he has the Word of God which is a defending and protecting weapon. The bible says THE WEAPONS OF OUR WARFARE ARE NOT CARNAL……

We also have weapons. One thing I want to bring to your attention is that the enemy cleverly forms their weapons. The bible says, "…*NO WEAPON THAT IS FORMED*……."

The word translated **FORMED** is from the Hebrew word "**YATSAR**" which means – to frame, create, be predetermined, plan, ordain, conceive, to mould, to squeeze into a shape. These meanings are pointing to the cleverness and trickiness of the enemy.

The enemy takes his time to plan against the righteous. The enemy is often very meticulous whilst the believer is trusting. Who wins a battle like that?

One key characteristic that cuts across all the channels – weapons, avenues or means – through which the enemy hurts people, is that they are well thought out. Well planned. The enemy would not just wake up and say I want to hurt this fellow today. No! Most likely it will take months if not years. In fact, some are predetermined before you were born.

When Haman was planning to wipe out the Jews, he had to consult an oracle to choose the date for the execution and extinction of the Jewish race (See Esther 9:24).

Some decisions made against you might have been made after consultations with demon goddess and spirit.

THE WEAPONS

Now let's see some of the weapons the enemy uses. I have added some specialised prayer points to counter and destroy each weapon. Make sure you pray the prayer points.

WEAPON 1: CURSES (NUMBERS 22:1-6)

And the children of Israel set forward, and pitched in the plains of Moab on this side Jordan by Jericho. And Balak the son of Zippor saw all that Israel had done to the Amorites. And Moab was sore afraid of the people, because they were many: and Moab was distressed because of the children of Israel. And Moab said unto the elders of Midian, Now shall this company lick up all that are round about us, as the ox licketh up the grass of the field. And Balak the son of Zippor was king of the Moabites at that time. He sent messengers therefore unto Balaam the son of Beor to Pethor, which is by the river of the land of the children of his people, to call him, saying, Behold, there is a people come out from Egypt: behold, they cover the face of the earth, and they abide over against me: ***COME NOW THEREFORE, I PRAY THEE, CURSE ME THIS PEOPLE; FOR THEY ARE TOO MIGHTY FOR ME: PERADVENTURE I SHALL PREVAIL, THAT WE MAY SMITE THEM, AND THAT I MAY DRIVE THEM OUT OF THE LAND:*** *for I wot that he whom thou blessest is blessed, and he whom thou cursest is cursed.* **NUM 22:1-6**

Bishop Oyedepo will always say, "…Wickedness is real". I will add that curses are also real. They must never be taken lightly because of a curse's ability to determine the happenings in a person's life.

What is a curse? A curse is the opposite of a blessing. A blessing is on the positive side of things or you could say a blessing is a positive force that attract goodness, mercy and favour to a person. A curse is on the negative side of things – ill lucks, disfavour and afflictions.

A blessing elongates, magnifies and adds something precious to a person's life. Whereas a curse reduces and takes away. A blessing protects. A curse exposes the victim to danger.

A curse is any form of desire that something evil/tragic will befall a person. This could either be spoken, written, imagined or thought about. Let's look at a few examples of curses in each of these categories.

CURSE – SPOKEN (Jer 22:28-30)

Is this man Coniah a despised broken idol? is he a vessel wherein is no pleasure? wherefore are they cast out, he and his seed, and are cast into a land which they know not? O earth, earth, earth, hear the word of the Lord. Thus saith the Lord, ***WRITE YE THIS MAN CHILDLESS, A MAN THAT SHALL NOT PROSPER IN HIS DAYS: FOR NO MAN OF HIS SEED SHALL PROSPER, SITTING UPON THE THRONE OF DAVID, AND RULING ANY MORE IN JUDAH.***

CURSE – WRITTEN (Col 2:14)

BLOTTING OUT THE HANDWRITING OF ORDINANCES THAT WAS AGAINST US, WHICH WAS CONTRARY TO US, AND TOOK IT OUT OF THE WAY, NAILING IT TO HIS CROSS.

CURSE – INWARD (Ps 62:4)

THEY ONLY CONSULT TO CAST HIM DOWN FROM HIS EXCELLENCY: THEY DELIGHT IN LIES: THEY BLESS WITH THEIR MOUTH, ***BUT THEY CURSE INWARDLY***

CURSE – IMAGINED (2Cor 10:4-5 & Ecc 10:20)

(FOR THE WEAPONS OF OUR WARFARE ARE NOT CARNAL, BUT MIGHTY THROUGH GOD TO THE PULLING DOWN OF STRONG HOLDS;) ***CASTING DOWN IMAGINATIONS***, AND EVERY HIGH THING THAT EXALTETH ITSELF AGAINST THE KNOWLEDGE OF GOD, ***AND BRINGING INTO CAPTIVITY EVERY THOUGHT TO THE OBEDIENCE OF CHRIST***

BALAK AND BALAAM

(See Numbers 22–25)

From the event that unfolded in the book of Number chapter 22 through 25. We see a weapon deployed against the children of Israel to hurt them.

The children of Israel were on their way to the promised land but they had to pass through the land of Moab. As soon as the whole nation heard and saw them coming, the bible says, "... *Moab was sore afraid of the people, because they were many: and Moab was distressed because of the children of Israel...* "

Their king – Balak – took to action to protect his people but with the wrong method. It is good that leaders know how to properly and righteously protect those they are leading in a way that wouldn't violate God's commandment. Balak went for protection in the wrong way. Leaders must learn how to use the power of God to protect themselves and those they are leading.

Balak sent for Balaam saying, ".... *behold, there is a people come out from Egypt: behold, they cover the face of the earth, and they abide over against me: come now therefore, I pray thee, curse me this people; for they are too mighty for me: peradventure I shall prevail, that we may smite them, and that I may drive them out of the land: for I wot that he whom thou blessest is blessed, and he whom thou cursest is cursed"* **Num 22:5-6**

He described the magnitude of the children of Israel. He was threatened by their numerical strength! Who says numbers don't scare the enemy. In the multitude of people is the king's honour – the more we are the better. There are people jealous of your achievement who are ready to do anything to bring you down, but thus says the Lord, "...NOTHING SHALL BY ANY MEANS HURT YOU".

Balak said to Balam, "*...I pray thee,* ***CURSE ME THIS PEOPLE; for THEY ARE TOO MIGHTY FOR ME: PERADVENTURE I SHALL PREVAIL, THAT WE MAY SMITE THEM, AND THAT I MAY***

DRIVE THEM OUT OF THE LAND: FOR I WOT THAT HE WHOM THOU BLESSEST IS BLESSED, AND HE WHOM THOU CURSEST IS CURSED".

Let's look closely at what Balak said. I called what he said a DEMONIC MISSION STATEMENT.

Firstly, he said,

"…. ***CURSE ME THIS PEOPLE….***"

This shows that there is no limit to the amount of people that can be placed under a curse. It also points to the different dimensions and operation of curses. A curse could be laid on one person or thousands of people at the same time which will produce the same result. Balak wanted everybody to partake of the curse, beginning from Moses to the least person in the camp.

Secondly, he said,

"….***for THEY ARE TOO MIGHTY FOR ME…***"

Balak knew he was no match for the children of Israel, so he wanted something to be done that will allow him – the whole nation of Moab – to overpower the Israelites. That was his mission. He was serious and ready to make it come to pass. If you read further, when Balaam told him the amount of animal he needed to buy he did not complain. He supplied whatever the "Chief Occultis" demanded.

Did you notice he said, "…**THEY ARE TOO MIGHTY FOR ME…**"? How did he know? What did he see? It is wise to know the forte of the enemy before engaging in a fight. When the strength of the opposition is known, it will help you prepare better. Many have lost battles because they couldn't discern the strength of the enemy and didn't prepare well.

Thirdly, Balak said,

> "…. ***PERADVENTURE I SHALL PREVAIL, THAT WE MAY SMITE THEM…***"

Balak wanted them cursed so that he might prevail over the Israelites. He wanted to win at all costs. He knew if he could have them cursed, they would lose their strength. Without strength, you can't win battles. Solomon said, *"If thou faint in the day of adversity,* **THY STRENGTH IS SMALL**" Prov 24:10

Have you lost your strength? A curse might be at work. A curse paralyses a person's effectiveness in every area of life. Balak said I don't mind fighting but only when they are in a position of DIMINISHED STRENGTH which is as a result of the curse. Fighting under a curse will engender defeat. Break the curse and win the battle.

He went on to say,

> "…***AND THAT I MAY DRIVE THEM OUT OF THE LAND…***"

Balak was very meticulous in his planning. He knew how to win the battle. He knew what to do to turn strong men into weaklings. He knew how to make owners beg for what was theirs in the first place. He was a master planner that knew it all. He knew the kind of association to get involved in so as to win the battle. He knew how to convince Balaam the chief Occultist. He gave Balaam a fat cheque and told him he will give him more if that was not enough.

The enemy is ready to go to any length to ensure evil befall their victim. Are you ready to go all the way for your victory? It will show in the price you are willing to pay. For Balak, the issue was not even the price, it was to see his desire over the children of Israel which is, "…***THAT I MAY DRIVE THEM OUT OF THE LAND…***"

I pray for you that the enemy will not drive you out of your possession. Any power assigned to do that is bound in the name of Jesus.

After he had smitten them, he will now be able to drive them out of the land. He knew he could not reverse the situation which is first, smite them and secondly, drive them out.

When people begin to lose grounds that rightfully belong to them, it is most likely that a curse is at work. A good example is a man who though makes the money for the family, the same man cannot confidently decide and determine the affairs of his home.

Balak's final statement was,

> "...***FOR I WOT THAT HE WHOM THOU BLESSEST IS BLESSED, AND HE WHOM THOU CURSEST IS CURSED***"

Balak had done the research to know who carried the anointing he needed to get results. He knew that Balaam was so in touch with heaven that whatever he says came to pass. The amplified version of the bible puts it this way, "*For I know [your reputation] that he whom you bless is blessed, and he whom you curse is cursed.*"

Balaam had a track record and Balak was aware of it. He knew that Balaam wouldn't miss because of his reputation. It is amazing how the wicked knows where to go to do their wicked works.

Friends, don't be deceived, there are strong deep demonic occultic men and women who have the power to curse and destroy. Whatever they say will come to pass, that is why a Christian must be VERY STRONG IN THE LORD AND THE POWER OF HIS MIGHT so you don't become a prey. Simeon the sorcerer is a good example (See Acts 8). We will talk more about Simeon when we discuss the weapon of Sorcery and Bewitchment.

JACOB AND HIS SONS
(GEN 49:1-4)

"*And Jacob called unto his sons, and said, Gather yourselves together,* ***THAT I MAY TELL YOU THAT WHICH SHALL BEFALL YOU IN THE LAST DAYS.*** *Gather yourselves together, and hear, ye sons of Jacob; and hearken unto Israel your father. Reuben, thou art my firstborn, my might, and the beginning of my strength, the excellency of dignity, and the excellency of power:* ***UNSTABLE AS WATER, THOU SHALT NOT EXCEL; BECAUSE THOU WENTEST UP TO THY FATHER'S BED; THEN DEFILEDST THOU IT: HE WENT UP TO MY COUCH***"

Jacob was about to die. He knew he had not finished his assignment, which was to define the future of his children. Fathers should know that we carry defining anointing and grace, that should be positively used for our children. You can define the future of your children by what you say to them.

Jacob said all his children should come so, "…**THAT I MAY TELL YOU THAT WHICH SHALL BEFALL YOU IN THE LAST DAYS…". ** This statement shows the heavy authority God has given to fathers. He had the effrontery to tell them what will happen to them in future. **FROM THAT POINT ON, IT CEASES TO BE FOR THEM BY THEIR OWN EFFORTS ALONE, THEIR LIVES IS BEEN SHAPED AND DESIGNED BY WHATEVER COMES OUT OF THE FATHER'S MOUTH** (THIS IS A SERIOUS STATEMENT, MEDITATE).

Never allow yourself to be cursed by a father figure, especially a man that has authority over you – fathers, mothers, school teachers, Men of God (especially your pastor or leader).

Reuben was the first born. He had great attributes and the future looked bright until the father cut him off by releasing curses on him. Curses cut a man off from his future (inheritance). Jacob described him as, "…**REUBEN, THOU ART MY FIRSTBORN, MY MIGHT,**

AND THE BEGINNING OF MY STRENGTH, THE EXCELLENCY OF DIGNITY, AND THE EXCELLENCY OF POWER…"

Can you imagine that, he had so much capacity and so much going for him? He was might, strength, dignity and excellence. That is all a man need to become great in life. Because he was the firstborn, he had the double portion reserved for him that he would enter into when the father dies, that too was taken from him and given to Joseph, a man with the blessing. Reuben's place was removed and Joseph's children - Ephraim and Manasseh - took it. Jacob said, "…*now* **THY TWO SONS, EPHRAIM AND MANASSEH, WHICH WERE BORN UNTO THEE IN THE LAND OF EGYPT BEFORE I CAME UNTO THEE INTO EGYPT, ARE MINE**; *as Reuben and Simeon,* **THEY SHALL BE MINE**. Gen 48:5

Jacob said they shall be mine as Reuben and Simeon, meaning they are now my biological sons just like Reuben and Simeon. They have the same inheritance as their uncles. At some point, the tribe of Reuben entered in scriptural obscurity. They never even settled in the promised land (See Numbers 32 & Judges 5). What their progenitor did, had an effect on them and how they settled down.

Anytime I teach or preach along this lines in our church, I tell our members to always ensure they get the blessing by all righteous means and avoid the curse at any cost. A curse is costly, you can't afford to pay the price.

CURSES HAVE REASONS

Did you realise that Jacob gave the reason why he had to place a curse on his first-born Reuben? The reason was, "**BECAUSE THOU WENTEST UP TO THY FATHER'S BED; THEN DEFILEDST THOU IT: HE WENT UP TO MY COUCH**".

Reuben slept with his father's wife. "*And it came to pass, when Israel dwelt in that land, that* ***Reuben went and lay with Bilhah his father's***

***concubine**: and Israel heard it. Now the sons of Jacob were twelve*". Gen 35:22

Whenever there is a legal ground, a curse will be attracted and stay because, "*As the bird by wandering, as the swallow by flying,* **SO THE CURSE CAUSELESS SHALL NOT COME**". Prov 26:2

When there is no cause, a curse can't be in operation.

WHAT CAUSES A CURSE?

I will show us based on the authority of the bible some things that can attract a curse.

1. Idol worship (Occultism & Witchcraft) – Ex 20:3-5; 34:14; 23:13, Deut 6:14.
2. False Religion – any religion that rejects the truth of the scripture is a false religion. 1John 2:18-24, 1John 4:3, 2John 1: 7-13.
3. Injustice to the weak and less privileged – Rom 15:1, Prov 11:26; 28:27.
4. Wrong behaviour towards Parents – Prov 20:20, Eph 6:1-3.
5. Anti-Semitism – Evil speaking and hatred for the Jewish people. Gen 12:3
6. Your own words – Prov 6:2, Ecc 5:6, Prov 18:21.
7. Words from Authority Figures such as fathers, mothers, teachers, husbands, pastors. Gen 31:32
8. Acts of wickedness – Prov 3:33; 24:24.

SUMMARY OF THE BLESSINGS AND THE CURSES IN DEUTERONOMY 28

The Blessings:

1. Being above and not beneath.
2. Prosperity or good success.
3. Being the head and not the tail.
4. Victory.
5. Health, or agility.
6. Reproductiveness.
7. Personal exaltation – divine promotion.

The Curses:

1. Being beneath and not above.
2. Poverty.
3. Being the tail and not the head.
4. Defeat or failure.
5. Sickness.
6. Inability to reproduce, or barrenness.
7. Humiliation.

How to break Curses?

1. You must know there is a curse in place.
2. Repent from every known act of ungodliness either by you or those related to you.
3. Renounce it.
4. Fight it off or break it. (James 4:7, Ps 107:2, Rev 12:11)

JOSHUA LAID A CURSE

(Joshua 6:26 & 1Kings 16:34)

AND JOSHUA ADJURED THEM AT THAT TIME, SAYING, CURSED BE THE MAN BEFORE THE LORD, THAT RISETH UP AND BUILDETH THIS CITY JERICHO: HE SHALL LAY THE FOUNDATION THEREOF IN HIS FIRSTBORN, AND IN HIS YOUNGEST SON SHALL HE SET UP THE GATES OF IT. Jos 6:26

IN HIS DAYS DID HIEL THE BETHELITE BUILD JERICHO: HE LAID THE FOUNDATION THEREOF IN ABIRAM HIS FIRSTBORN, AND SET UP THE GATES THEREOF IN HIS YOUNGEST SON SEGUB, ACCORDING TO THE WORD OF THE LORD, WHICH HE SPAKE BY JOSHUA THE SON OF NUN. 1Kings 16:34

God has just given the children of Israel victory that was led by Joshua against the land of Jericho. Afterwards, he released some words – in the form of a curse – that, "...*CURSED BE THE MAN BEFORE THE LORD, THAT RISETH UP AND BUILDETH THIS CITY JERICHO: HE SHALL LAY THE FOUNDATION THEREOF IN HIS FIRSTBORN, AND IN HIS YOUNGEST SON SHALL HE SET UP THE GATES OF IT*".

Joshua was declaring what will happen to the person that rises up to rebuild the wall of Jericho. Many years down the line – about 500 years – a man rose up called Hiel. He rebuilt the wall and suffered a great deal of consequence as pronounced by the man of God – Joshua.

His children died as Joshua said. *HE SHALL LAY THE FOUNDATION THEREOF IN HIS FIRSTBORN, AND IN HIS YOUNGEST SON SHALL HE SET UP THE GATES OF IT.* The two boys died accordingly. They were not sick, they just died because their father was careless and became involved with what he was not supposed to.

This curse came to pass 500 years after Joshua spoke it. This will show you how strong a curse can travel and be fulfilled if not broken by the power of God through serious deliverance ministrations.

Fathers must be careful about their actions as it can impact on their children. Look closely at this case. It wasn't the children that offended but they paid for it with their lives. It is therefore possible to pay for what you didn't buy. I pray for you that any agenda of darkness to make you pay for what you never bought shall scatter.

As I conclude this chapter, you need to remember that a curse can kill, reduce the future, stagnate and make one lose in life.

PRAYER AGAINST THE WEAPON OF CURSES

1. I break the power of any curse laid against me in the name of Jesus
2. Any generational curse working in my lineage, I destroy you in the name of Jesus.
3. I plead the blood of Jesus against any effect of any curse on my life.
4. The consuming fire, consume every curse upon my life.
5. I declare that by the finished work of Christ I am redeemed from any curse.
6. From now on, I walk in the blessing and not the curse.
7. The blessing of Abraham is mine. I reject the curse of Egypt.
8. Any one in my family that will take the wrong step for any curse to be released into my life shall not take such steps.
9. Curses waiting to come to pass in my life are destroyed in the name of Jesus.
10. No weapon of curse formed against me will ever prosper. Amen

MAKE THIS CONFESSION OUT LOUD

It is written that Christ has redeemed me from the curse of the law. He became a curse for me so as to receive the blessing. Let the redeemed of the Lord say so, I say so because I am redeemed. I repent from every sin, personal and generational that is allowing the devil to have access to me. I plead the blood against it now and I command the effect of such curse to be neutralised in the name of Jesus. Let God arise and every curse be broken, curses that are spoken, imagined, written, thought of inwardly against be destroyed now by the consuming fire of God. I destroy the curses effecting sickness, poverty, accident, weakness, misfortune in the name of Jesus. I paralyse them all. I am covered in the blood of Jesus, from henceforth let no man trouble me because I bear in my body the mark of the Lord Jesus. Amen

(See Gal 3:13-14; Ps 107:2; Rev 12:11; Heb 2:3)

WEAPON 2: SORCERY (Acts 8: 9-11)

But there was a certain man, called Simon, which beforetime in **THE SAME CITY USED SORCERY,** *and* **BEWITCHED THE PEOPLE OF SAMARIA,** *giving out that himself was some great one: To whom they all gave heed, from the least to the greatest, saying: This man is the great power of God. And to him they had regard,* **BECAUSE THAT OF LONG TIME HE HAD BEWITCHED THEM WITH SORCERIES.**

The second weapon we will look at is the weapon of sorcery. A sorcerer is a person that uses sorcery. The word sorcery is from the Greek word "MAGEUO" which is where we get the word magic. A sorcerer is therefore a magician or someone involved in magical arts. There is no innocent magician. They are all demonic in origin and operation. Do not let yourself be deceived. Anywhere you see a magician, you have found a sorcerer. You have seen somebody that can talk to spirit and conjure them to do things for him.

Sorcery can be defined as the art, practices, or spells of a person who exercises supernatural powers through the aid of evil spirits. In the class of sorcerers, you will find enchanters, diviners, warlock, star gazers and readers, necromancers, mediums, witches, wizards, and occultic grandmasters. I will elaborate more on some of these, though they have some similarities, their activities can at times be different.

From the text – Acts 8:9-11 – we see a man called Simon who was a sorcerer. He used what the bible called sorcery, which we saw earlier is from the MAGIC root word. I believe that Simon would have had to display some level of power and pull some stunts before the crowd. I see Simon as a man who had magic shows on some particular day, maybe Wednesday. Every Wednesday, the people gathered before him and he displayed. He got into action and by so doing the bible says, **"...HE BEWITCHED THE PEOPLE OF SAMARIA, GIVING OUT THAT HIMSELF WAS SOME GREAT ONE...".**

The word translated "Bewitched" is from the Greek word

"EXISTEMI" which literally means – to throw out of position, to displace, throw into wonderment (how could he have thrown a whole city of Samaria into wonder if he wasn't performing some sort of wonder or magic)., To be out of one's mind, besides one's self, to be insane (Insanity is not only when someone runs mad but also when you can't think straight, normal and logical).

He bewitched them against logical reasoning. Bewitchment works mainly on the mind. Whenever you see a man who can't accept or function by the truth or see the truth, he's possibly bewitched. His mind is under the influence of demonic powers. That is why a man can move out of a house he bought with his money and move in with a strange woman and be paying rent.

Simon bewitched Samaria and also told them what to think and how to relate with him. He said he was a great person and everybody in the city obeyed him. No one could question him. Is there anyone around you that you can't righteously and sincerely ask questions? That person might have bewitched you.

There are men who walk in the sorcery and bewitchment power. You can't approach them, before you get to them, you either change your mind or forget what your intentions were. If this is your case, lay your hand on your head now and let the power of God move into action. I take authority over sorcery and bewitchment in your life. Be free now in the name of Jesus. I break that evil hold by the blood of Jesus.

MOSES AND THE EGYPTIAN SORCERERS
(Ex 7:10-12)

AND MOSES AND AARON WENT IN UNTO PHARAOH, AND THEY DID SO AS THE LORD HAD COMMANDED: AND AARON CAST DOWN HIS ROD BEFORE PHARAOH, AND BEFORE HIS SERVANTS, AND IT BECAME A SERPENT. ***THEN PHARAOH ALSO CALLED THE WISE MEN AND THE SORCERERS:*** *NOW* ***THE MAGICIANS OF EGYPT, THEY ALSO DID IN LIKE***

MANNER WITH THEIR ENCHANTMENTS. *FOR THEY CAST DOWN EVERY MAN HIS ROD, AND THEY BECAME SERPENTS: BUT AARON'S ROD SWALLOWED UP THEIR RODS.*

Moses had to confront some powers of darkness in Egypt. He had been visited by God and sent to deliver the children of Israel. He was adequately prepared by God for the fight ahead. God doesn't send into Egypt without first preparing you for Egypt!

He got there and displayed the first miracle, shockingly the Occultic grandmaster in the cabinet of Pharaoh was also ready and able to perform. The bible says, "...*AARON CAST DOWN HIS ROD BEFORE PHARAOH, AND BEFORE HIS SERVANTS, AND IT BECAME A SERPENT.* ***THEN PHARAOH ALSO CALLED THE WISE MEN AND THE SORCERERS:*** *NOW* ***THE MAGICIANS OF EGYPT, THEY ALSO DID IN LIKE MANNER WITH THEIR ENCHANTMENTS.*** *FOR THEY CAST DOWN EVERY MAN HIS ROD, AND THEY BECAME SERPENTS".*

Aaron cast down his rod and by the power of God it became a serpent. The bible says that Pharaoh called a particular set of people, "...**THE WISE MEN** and **THE SORCERERS**... **THE MAGICIANS**... they also did in like manner".

The WISE MEN: In Hebrew "**CHAKAM**"

Literal meaning is skilful, shrewd, crafty (where we get WITCH**CRAFT** from), subtle and cunning.

The SORCERERS: In Hebrew **"KASHAPH"**

Means to practice or use witchcraft

The MAGICIANS: In Hebrew **"CHARTOM"**

It means diviner, astrologer, engraver, horoscopist (checking your horoscope is satanic and wrong), drawer or writer of magical lines and circles which is gotten by occultic knowledge.

These were the categories of men Pharaoh beckoned on when the battle was hot. These men did exactly what Aaron did by the power of

God. Anybody who tells you the Devil has no power is either ignorant or an agent of the Devil himself.

THEY ALSO DID IN LIKE MANNER WITH THEIR ENCHANTMENTS

Did you notice that the bible says these men – wise Men, Magician and Sorcerers – did likewise? They did exactly what Aaron did – rod turns to serpent. They did it with demonic power and the bible says it was by ENCHANTMENTS. This weapon of enchantment we shall consider shortly.

Paul in the New Testament mentioned some of the names of these Sorcerers. He said, *"NOW AS **JANNES AND JAMBRES WITHSTOOD MOSES,** SO DO THESE ALSO RESIST THE TRUTH: MEN OF CORRUPT MINDS, REPROBATE CONCERNING THE FAITH. BUT THEY SHALL PROCEED NO FURTHER: FOR THEIR FOLLY SHALL BE MANIFEST UNTO ALL MEN, AS THEIR'S ALSO WAS".* **2TIM 3: 8-9**

These men – Jannes and Jambres – are highly occultic, charmers, wizards that used sorcery in Egypt. Their exploits gave Pharaoh confidence to challenge divine instructions. Paul said they, "…**WITHSTOOD MOSES**…" that means they opposed all what Moses said and did., They gave Moses a hard time, though we didn't see or read much of these men in the Old Testament. Paul, in the New Testament shed a little light on their atrocities.

Paul, writing by the Holy Ghost said something shocking. He said the activities of such men – Jannes and Jambres – will increase and this is a sign on Perilous time. Let me show you the character of these Sorcerers.

CHARACTERS OF JANNES AND JAMBRES

"…SO DO THESE ALSO RESIST THE TRUTH: MEN OF CORRUPT MINDS, REPROBATE CONCERNING THE FAITH. BUT THEY

SHALL PROCEED NO FURTHER: FOR THEIR FOLLY SHALL BE MANIFEST UNTO ALL MEN, AS THEIR'S ALSO WAS... "

1. They resist – oppose, take a stand or position, set themselves against, mount a guard against – the truth. (It's amazing what some people are willing and ready to do against the truth).
2. Men of corrupt minds.
3. Reprobate – not standing the test – concerning the faith. (They behave in an immoral way).
4. They are foolish men.

DIVINE JUDGEMENT ON JANNES AND JAMBRES

"*...BUT THEY SHALL PROCEED NO FURTHER: FOR THEIR FOLLY SHALL BE MANIFEST UNTO ALL MEN, AS THEIR'S ALSO WAS*".

1. They shall proceed no further, i.e. their activities shall come to a stop. Their movements shall meet with frustration.
2. Their shame will appear to all. Jannes and Jambres were openly disgraced when Aaron's rod, turned serpent swallowed their snakes. Every sorcerer assigned against you shall be openly disgraced.

PRAYERS AGAINST THE WEAPON OF SORCERERS AND SORCERY

1. Any sorcerer hired to work against me, I cancel and frustrate your agenda.
2. Magicians in my environment, I render your powers useless in Jesus name.
3. As Jannes and Jambres withstood Moses, anyone assigned to stand against my advancement shall be openly disgraced like Jannes and Jambres in Jesus name.
4. Occultic Witchcraft using sorceries against my destiny, I command you to be consumed by fire in Jesus name.
5. You sorcerer in charge of my case receives madness now in Jesus name.
6. Incantation of the sorcerers shall not work against me and my family.
7. I barricade my life with the fire of God.
8. Weapons of sorcerers shall not prosper over me in Jesus name.
9. No weapon formed against me shall prosper.
10. Nothing shall by any means hurt me.
11. Angel of the living God, go forth and kill every sorcerer that has been paid to kill me.

WEAPON 3: DIVINATION AND ENCHANTMENT
(Num 23:23 & Ez 21:21-22)

Surely there is no enchantment against Jacob, neither is there any divination against Israel: according to this time it shall be said of Jacob and of Israel, What hath God wrought! **Numbers 23:23**

FOR THE KING OF BABYLON STOOD AT THE PARTING OF THE WAY, AT THE HEAD OF THE TWO WAYS, TO USE DIVINATION: he made his arrows bright, he consulted with images, he looked in the liver. At his **RIGHT HAND WAS THE DIVINATION FOR JERUSALEM,** to appoint captains, to open the mouth in the slaughter, to lift up the voice with shouting, to appoint battering rams against the gates, to cast a mount, and to build a fort. **Ez 21:21-22**

FOR THE KING OF BABYLON STANDS AT THE PARTING OF THE WAY, AT THE FORK OF THE TWO WAYS, **TO USE DIVINATION**. HE SHAKES THE ARROWS, HE CONSULTS THE TERAPHIM (HOUSEHOLD IDOLS), HE LOOKS AT THE LIVER [OF AN ANIMAL FOR AN OMEN]. IN HIS RIGHT HAND IS THE LOT MARKED FOR JERUSALEM: TO SET BATTERING RAMS, TO OPEN THE MOUTH CALLING FOR DESTRUCTION, TO LIFT UP THE VOICE WITH A WAR CRY, TO SET BATTERING RAMS AGAINST THE GATES, TO PUT UP ASSAULT RAMPS, AND TO BUILD SIEGE WALLS. **Ez 21:21-22 (AMP)**

These two-powerful demonic weapons often go together, so I have decided to address them together. They are different in operation.

I found these two definitions of Divination from google. Firstly, divination is from a Latin word "divinare" which means "to foresee, to be inspired by a god". Divination is the attempt to gain insight into a question or situation by way of an occultic, standardized process or ritual.

Secondly, divination is known as the art or practice that seeks to foresee or foretell future events or discover hidden knowledge usually by the interpretation of omens or by the aid of supernatural powers.

From the account of Prophet Ezekiel, he was divinely granted to know that Babylon was coming with war but before that, he also saw behind the scene to know exactly how the King of Babylon was making his plans. He saw, "...**THE KING OF BABYLON STOOD AT THE PARTING OF THE WAY, AT THE HEAD OF THE TWO WAYS, TO USE DIVINATION...**"

The King of Babylon took a particular and specific position and location – THE PARTING OF THE WAY, THE HEAD OF TWO WAYS – to device his divination agenda. The occultic people knows how to use locations, signs, seasons, event, herbs to do evil. Who told him that he should go and invoke the spirit at the head of two ways? He also had instruments of divination, "...he made his arrows bright, he consulted with images, he looked in the liver...".

The Amplified version put more light to it, "HE SHAKES THE ARROWS, HE CONSULTS THE TERAPHIM (HOUSEHOLD IDOLS), HE LOOKS AT THE LIVER [OF AN ANIMAL FOR AN OMEN] (*Omen is an event seen as a sign of good or bad*).

INSTRUMENTS OF DIVINATION

1. Arrows.
2. Images or Teraphim – household Idols (Babylonian and Roman gods) (Judges 17:5; 2Kings 23:24).
3. Liver of an animal for an omen.
4. Cup – Gen 44:2,5 & 15.
5. Water.
6. Sand.
7. Ifa Oracle - It is called Opele by the Yorubas, a tribe in Nigeria.

ENCHANTMENT

"Surely there is no enchantment against Jacob....".

Enchantment is defined as the state of been under a magical spell. Under an overpowering influence or spirit. The Hebrew word for enchantment is "NACHASH" it means INCANTATION.

Enchantment is the thread that weaves it all together – witchcraft, sorcery, divination, magic, medium, occultic grandmaster. What they do to perform their evil work is to ENCHANT or recite incantations.

You remember when the wise men, sorcerer and magician were called to do exactly what Aaron had done by the power of God: turning a rod into a serpent. The three categories of men were said to "...ALSO DID IN LIKE MANNER **WITH THEIR ENCHANTMENTS...**"

They knew what to say or recite. The process of them saying those words is called enchantment. The words are called incantations. You know this is not a joke when a man knows what to say and a stick will turn to a serpent. In fact, when Aaron's rod turned into a serpent, he didn't have to say anything. He just obeyed a divine instruction – throw down your rod.

But when the wise men, magicians and sorcerers got on the scene, they displayed demonic power. Just like the prophet of Baal had tried to bring fire down, but they failed. God judged them. Here, God allowed the incantation to work for a reason – to harden Pharaoh's mind.

That is why you need to wage war against enchanters and their incantation. You need to pray that fire consumes their memory as they enchant against you.

PRAYERS AGAINST THE WEAPON OF DIVINATION AND ENCHANTMENT (INCANTATION)

1. God who makes diviners mad, I command that you make mad anyone divining evil against me in Jesus name (Is 44:25)
2. Instruments of divination set in motion against me is destroyed by the blood of Jesus.
3. I decree that diviners shall be deceived by their own instrument in Jesus name.
4. Fire of God destroy the enchanters and diviners searching out my glory.
5. Father, in the name of Jesus, please defend your interest in my life.
6. Kings of the earth assigned to wage war against me by divination, I command you to be paralysed.
7. Oh God, scatter the language of every diviner and enchanters.
8. I command blindness for a season over any diviner mentioning my name in Jesus name. Acts 13:6-11
9. Enemies of righteousness in my affairs, receive the judgement of God.
10. Hand of God, come upon every diviner, sorcerer, magician for evil in Jesus name.

WEAPON 4: WISE MEN (Ex 7:11; Esther 1:13 & Mat 2:1-9)

THEN PHARAOH ALSO CALLED THE WISE MEN AND THE SORCERERS: NOW THE MAGICIANS OF EGYPT, THEY ALSO DID IN LIKE MANNER WITH THEIR ENCHANTMENTS. EX 7:11

THEN THE KING SAID TO THE WISE MEN, WHICH KNEW THE TIMES, (FOR SO WAS THE KING'S MANNER TOWARD ALL THAT KNEW LAW AND JUDGMENT. ESTHER 1:13

"NOW WHEN JESUS WAS BORN IN BETHLEHEM OF JUDAEA IN THE DAYS OF HEROD THE KING, BEHOLD, ***THERE CAME WISE MEN FROM THE EAST*** *TO JERUSALEM, SAYING, WHERE IS HE THAT IS BORN KING OF THE JEWS? FOR WE HAVE SEEN HIS STAR IN THE EAST, AND ARE COME TO WORSHIP HIM…AND THOU BETHLEHEM, IN THE LAND OF JUDA, ART NOT THE LEAST AMONG THE PRINCES OF JUDA: FOR OUT OF THEE SHALL COME A GOVERNOR, THAT SHALL RULE MY PEOPLE ISRAEL. THEN HEROD,* ***WHEN HE HAD PRIVILY CALLED THE WISE MEN****, ENQUIRED OF THEM DILIGENTLY WHAT TIME THE STAR APPEARED. AND HE SENT THEM TO BETHLEHEM, AND SAID, GO AND SEARCH DILIGENTLY FOR THE YOUNG CHILD; AND WHEN YE HAVE FOUND HIM, BRING ME WORD AGAIN, THAT I MAY COME AND WORSHIP HIM ALSO. WHEN THEY HAD HEARD THE KING,* ***THEY DEPARTED; AND, LO, THE STAR, WHICH THEY SAW IN THE EAST, WENT BEFORE THEM, TILL IT CAME AND STOOD OVER WHERE THE YOUNG CHILD WAS.***" MAT 2:1-2 & 6-9

The fourth weapon we will be looking at is the weapon the bible calls the "Wise Men". These are men with ancient demonic wisdom who know how to read times, seasons and especially stars.

These are men that if you follow their counsel, you will always get results. They are called by different names in different countries. They don't appear to be harmful, they seem harmless most of the time but their source is strongly demonic and is evil. They have wonderful and sweet sayings though.

These are men who know what ordinary men don't know. They have supernatural demonic insight into situations. They seem to have a solution for men at their fingertips.

SOLOMON'S WISDOM COMPARED WITH SOME WISE MEN

And Solomon's wisdom excelled the wisdom of all the children of the east country, and all the wisdom of Egypt. ***For he was wiser than all men; than Ethan the Ezrahite, and Heman, and Chalcol, and Darda, the sons of Mahol:*** *and his fame was in all nations round about.* **1Kings 4:30-31.**

God gave Solomon wisdom which he used in leading Israel when he was the king, but the bible says there were some people who had been around before him. Notable men, in fact, they are referred to as WISE MEN from THE EAST. The east here is a pagan and as part of their religion, they paid a special attention to the study of stars and gained an international reputation for astrology.

This is confirmed in the story of Jesus, when he was born. We read that some wise men came from the east. They said, "…WHERE IS HE THAT IS BORN KING OF THE JEWS? **FOR WE HAVE SEEN HIS STAR IN THE EAST**, AND ARE COME TO WORSHIP HIM…"

These men were in the east, and they knew what happened in Bethlehem, Judaea which was thousands of miles away! How did they know? The wise men said, "…**FOR WE HAVE SEEN HIS STAR IN THE EAST…**" They saw the star in the east, probably from their house. They looked outside and noticed a different kind of star in the sky and did more research to ascertain that it was the star of a King. The wise men are star readers, gazers, astrologers, teachers and interpreters of dark sayings.

From this incident, we can conclude that someone can be in Asia and be monitoring the star in Asia of a person who resides in Europe. And if the person monitoring in Asia want to know where and what the person in Europe is doing, all he has to do is follow the star. The wise men said, "*When they had heard the king, they departed; and, lo,* ***the star, which they saw in the east, went before them, till it came and stood over where the young child was.*** *When they saw the star, they rejoiced with exceeding great joy*" **Mat 2:9-10**

They followed Jesus' star until it came to the exact place where he was. That means you can be located and traced by your star. The wise men doesn't need to know your physical address, they just need to locate your star and the star will tell them when you were born – HEROD ENQUIRED WHEN THE STAR APPEARED (Mat 2:7). If Herod could ask that, who knows what the enemy is asking about you. Anyone asking questions about you in order to hurt you shall be put to shame.

QUEEN VASHTI LOST THE THRONE

Queen Vashti was a celebrated queen who lost her throne because she disobeyed the king's instruction. Not knowing what to do and how to go about this situation. King Ahasuerus said, "*. . . to the wise men, which knew the times, (for so was the king's manner toward all that knew law and judgment: And the next unto him was Carshena, Shethar, Admatha, Tarshish, Meres, Marsena, and Memucan, the seven princes of Persia and Media, which saw the king's face, and which sat the first in the kingdom;)* ***WHAT SHALL WE DO UNTO THE QUEEN VASHTI*** *according to law, because she hath not performed the commandment of the king Ahasuerus by the chamberlains. . .* " **Esther 1:13-15**.

The answer of one of the wise men called Memucan knocked queen Vashti out of the palace forever and she became an ordinary citizen without honour. This is one of the major assignment of the wise men – to cast men down from their excellency using the means of demonic counsels.

Memucan said to the king, "… *Vashti the queen hath not done wrong to the king only, but also to all the princes, and to all the people that are in all the provinces of the king Ahasuerus. For this deed of the queen shall come abroad unto all women, so that they shall despise their husbands in their eyes, when it shall be reported. The king Ahasuerus commanded Vashti the queen to be brought in before him, but she came not. Likewise shall the ladies of Persia and Media say this day unto all the king's princes, which have heard of the deed of the queen. Thus shall there arise too much contempt and wrath.* **IF IT PLEASE THE KING, LET THERE GO A ROYAL COMMANDMENT FROM HIM, AND LET IT BE WRITTEN AMONG THE LAWS OF THE PERSIANS AND THE MEDES, THAT IT BE NOT ALTERED, THAT VASHTI COME NO MORE BEFORE KING AHASUERUS; AND LET THE KING GIVE HER ROYAL ESTATE UNTO ANOTHER THAT IS BETTER THAN SHE. AND WHEN THE KING'S DECREE WHICH HE SHALL MAKE SHALL BE PUBLISHED THROUGHOUT ALL HIS EMPIRE, (FOR IT IS GREAT,) ALL THE WIVES SHALL GIVE TO THEIR HUSBAND'S HONOUR, BOTH TO GREAT AND SMALL.**" Esther 1:16-20

By one man's counsel, a highly-respected person became a person of low degree. From wealth, she went to poverty and from fame to shame. Memucan's counsel totally destroyed Vashti, he said to the king that this is what you must do, firstly, you have to marry another person to replace the proud Vashti. Secondly, he told the king that the decision must be noised abroad so that all the women will learn not to misbehave to their husband.

Somehow, this demonic wise man had an unusual insight into what had happened and was able to bring a solution.

DAVID'S PRAYER AGAINST AHITHOPHEL

David was in the midst of a family battle, his son, Absalom had risen against him to kill him and take the throne. At this point, David was on the run. Some came and told him that Ahithophel had joined force with Absalom to bring him down. David moved straight into action, which I advise you to always do. Never let battle linger on without addressing it. Mummy Oyenike Areogun will always say that the warfare you should fight today, don't fight it tomorrow. Fight now!

As soon as David had that information see what he did, *"And one told David, saying, Ahithophel is among the conspirators with Absalom.* **AND DAVID SAID, O LORD, I PRAY THEE, TURN THE COUNSEL OF AHITHOPHEL INTO FOOLISHNESS.**" 2Sam 15:31

David knew the kind of anointing Ahithophel had, in fact, it was said concerning Ahithophel that, "...**THE COUNSEL OF AHITHOPHEL, WHICH HE COUNSELLED IN THOSE DAYS, WAS AS IF A MAN HAD ENQUIRED AT THE ORACLE OF GOD**: *so was all the counsel of Ahithophel both with David and with Absalom.* 2Sam 16:23.

When he gives a counsel, it was as if God Himself was counselling you, so you will never go wrong. David knew how many battles he had won because of the counsel of Ahithophel. When we read that David never lost a battle, it is because he had men like Ahithophel who knew what accurate steps to be taken.

Once Ahithophel changed camp from David to Absalom, he knew he had to pray because now the wisdom God gave Ahithophel had been hijacked by the Devil. He prayed, "O Lord... turn the counsel – advice, wisdom – of Ahithophel into foolishness".

God answered the prayer and for the first time, the counsel of Ahithophel was not followed though that was the best and only counsel that would have led to the defeat and destruction of David's kingdom. "And Hushai said unto Absalom, the counsel that Ahithophel hath given is not good at this time... And Absalom and all the men of Israel said, The counsel of Hushai the Archite is better than the counsel of Ahithophel. **FOR THE LORD HAD APPOINTED TO DEFEAT THE GOOD COUNSEL OF AHITHOPHEL**, to the intent that the Lord might bring evil upon Absalom.... **AND WHEN AHITHOPHEL SAW THAT HIS COUNSEL WAS NOT FOLLOWED**, he saddled his ass, and arose, and gat him home to his house, to his city, and put his household in order, **AND HANGED HIMSELF, AND DIED, AND WAS BURIED IN THE SEPULCHRE OF HIS FATHER**" 2Sam 17:7,14 & 23.

He died because David prayed on time. Don't just pray, learn to quickly pray! If you delay in praying you may loose the battle God ordained that you win. Never slack, get into action.

I see God releasing upon you grace for prompt actions against the enemy. Amen

PRAYERS AGAINST THE WEAPON OF WISE MEN

1. Lord, turn the counsel of evil wise men concerning me into foolishness.
2. Let foolishness cover every wise man hired against me as a mantle.
3. I command confusion in the camp of my enemies.
4. Let every wise man hired to bring me down fall by their own hands.
5. Evil consultants and consultation is declared null and void.
6. Holy ghost fire, locate and destroy the occultic men issuing evil advice about me in Jesus name.
7. Wise men monitoring my star, receive blindness in Jesus name.
8. Wise men monitoring my star and location, receive confusion in Jesus name.
9. I crush the weapon of evil wise men against me and my family.
10. No weapon of evil wise men will hurt me, neither will it prosper in my life in Jesus name.
11. Evil conspiracy of wise men, scatter now in Jesus name.
12. Wise men assigned to naked me shall be disgraced.
13. I decree open shame is the portion of every wise men targeting me for evil in Jesus name. Amen

WEAPON 5: THE SPIRT OF HEROD (MAT 2:1, 3-5, 7-8,13 & 16. ACTS 12:1-6 & 12)

"NOW WHEN JESUS WAS BORN IN BETHLEHEM OF JUDAEA IN THE DAYS OF HEROD THE KING, BEHOLD, THERE CAME WISE MEN FROM THE EAST TO JERUSALEM… WHEN HEROD THE KING HAD HEARD THESE THINGS, HE WAS TROUBLED, AND ALL JERUSALEM WITH HIM. AND WHEN HE HAD GATHERED ALL THE CHIEF PRIESTS AND SCRIBES OF THE PEOPLE TOGETHER, ***HE DEMANDED OF THEM WHERE CHRIST SHOULD BE BORN****. AND THEY SAID UNTO HIM, IN BETHLEHEM OF JUDAEA: FOR THUS IT IS WRITTEN BY THE PROPHET… THEN HEROD,* ***WHEN HE HAD PRIVILY CALLED THE WISE MEN, ENQUIRED OF THEM DILIGENTLY WHAT TIME THE STAR APPEARED****. AND HE SENT THEM TO BETHLEHEM, AND SAID,* ***GO AND SEARCH DILIGENTLY FOR THE YOUNG CHILD****; AND WHEN YE HAVE FOUND HIM, BRING ME WORD AGAIN, THAT I MAY COME AND WORSHIP HIM ALSO… AND WHEN THEY WERE DEPARTED, BEHOLD, THE ANGEL OF THE LORD APPEARETH TO JOSEPH IN A DREAM, SAYING, ARISE, AND TAKE THE YOUNG CHILD AND HIS MOTHER, AND FLEE INTO EGYPT, AND BE THOU THERE UNTIL I BRING THEE WORD:* ***FOR HEROD WILL SEEK THE YOUNG CHILD TO DESTROY HIM****…* ***THEN HEROD****, WHEN HE SAW THAT HE WAS MOCKED OF THE WISE MEN, WAS EXCEEDING WROTH, AND SENT FORTH,* ***AND SLEW ALL THE CHILDREN*** *THAT WERE IN BETHLEHEM, AND IN ALL THE COASTS THEREOF, FROM TWO YEARS OLD AND UNDER,* ***ACCORDING TO THE TIME WHICH HE HAD DILIGENTLY INQUIRED*** *OF THE WISE MEN".* **Mat 2:1, 3-5, 7-8, 13 & 16**

This weapon – the spirit of Herod – is used by the enemy against the rising stars, against the glory of little children. The spirit of Herod is the spirit that destroys good things in infancy. Jesus had been born and Herod was the king at the time, when he heard that another king is born, bible said he became, "...TROUBLED, AND ALL JERUSALEM WITH HIM..." the question is why should Herod and the whole Jerusalem be troubled because a child has just been born. The reason is the identity of the child was declared from the beginning. The wise men said he is the king of the Jews and they had come to worship him.

Herod had been king for many years, perhaps no one came even from the next village to worship him, but here are wise men from the East – thousands of miles away – who came to worship him. Immediately, envy, jealousy and rivalry set him. When men are envious they can do anything.

The spirit of Herod is a spirit that wants it all to himself – you are a king already and another king has just been born, is that a crime? That is the spirit that says I am the only person here and any other person that wants to rise up will be cut down. If you find yourself serving under such a person who has this spirit, you have a serious warfare to fight. This is the reason some senior pastor wouldn't give some platforms to some younger minister because the senior man is a Herod! He hates rising stars.

The bible recorded that Herod kept on enquiring, demanding, asking, finding and looking for information about Jesus. "...***HE DEMANDED*** *OF THEM WHERE CHRIST SHOULD BE BORN... WHEN HE HAD PRIVILY CALLED THE WISE MEN,* ***ENQUIRED OF THEM DILIGENTLY*** *WHAT TIME THE STAR APPEARED...* ***GO AND SEARCH DILIGENTLY*** *FOR THE YOUNG CHILD...*" And when Herod was ready to unleash his attack on Jesus it was done, "***ACCORDING TO THE TIME WHICH HE HAD DILIGENTLY INQUIRED OF THE WISE MEN***".

Did you notice those phrases?

1. He demanded.
2. He enquired diligently.

3. Go and search diligently or thoroughly.

And finally, he executed his plans according to the time which he had diligently – carefully and thoroughly – inquired of the wise men.

The details Herod was asking wasn't for fun, he needed them to know what move to take. The enemy can't attack you successfully without first having some level of information about you. It through you giving it out or them seeking it by any other means. This is the reason you must be discreet. Not everybody has the right to know what is going on in your life, you are better off keeping some things to yourself.

There are parents who instead of protecting their children expose them to all manner of people. They give out information about their children to someone who is probably envious of them. I also do not understand the madness some people do that is called "Baby shower". A baby has not yet come, you have called all the witches who probably never wished you well to come and celebrate with you. You have called them to come and eat your unborn child. There are those who also flood the social media with unnecessary information of themselves. This is a sign of foolishness! Friends you don't only need prayer against the spirit of Herod, you need wisdom. The angel gave Joseph what steps to take - *ARISE, AND TAKE THE YOUNG CHILD AND HIS MOTHER, AND FLEE INTO EGYPT, AND BE THOU THERE UNTIL I BRING THEE WORD…*" Because, "*…HEROD WILL SEEK THE YOUNG CHILD TO DESTROY HIM…*".

HEROD AND THE APOSTLE

"Now about that time **HEROD THE KING STRETCHED FORTH HIS HANDS TO VEX CERTAIN OF THE CHURCH. AND HE KILLED JAMES THE BROTHER OF JOHN WITH THE SWORD**. And because he saw it pleased the Jews, **HE PROCEEDED FURTHER TO TAKE PETER ALSO**. (Then were the days of unleavened bread.) And when he had apprehended him, he put him in prison, and delivered him to four quaternions of soldiers to keep him; intending after Easter to bring him forth to the people. Peter therefore was kept in prison: but prayer was made without ceasing of the church unto God for him. And when Herod would have brought him forth, the same night Peter was sleeping between two soldiers, bound with two chains: and the keepers before the door kept the prison… And when Peter was come to himself, he said, Now I know of a surety, **THAT THE LORD HATH SENT HIS ANGEL, AND HATH DELIVERED ME OUT OF THE HAND OF HEROD**, and from all the expectation of the people of the Jews" **Acts 12:1-6 & 11**

We see in this account that the spirit of Herod is a spirit that fights those with Apostolic callings.

He killed James the brother of John with the sword.

This is one of the major anti gospel sprit, it fights the expansion of the Church. Everyone involved in Church work must know how to arrest the operation of this spirit. If you read the whole chapter of Acts twelve, you will realise that it was the power of consistent fervent prayer that delivered Peter out of the hands of Herod.

PRAYERS AGAINST THE SPIRIT OF HEROD

1. Hand of Herod over my life, wither in Jesus name
2. Herod of my father's house that is looking to cut me short, I cut you off in Jesus name.
3. Herod boasting against me, receive angelic slap now in Jesus name.
4. I am delivered out of the hands of Herod in Jesus name.
5. Spirit of Herod fighting my calling, I scatter you by fire in Jesus name.
6. Any spirit assigned to release sword amongst my church, family, business is bound in Jesus name.
7. Spirit of Herod planning open disgrace for me, I arrest you in the name of Jesus.
8. Angel of the living God, deliver me from evil expectation in Jesus name.
9. I take authority over any spirit assigned against the glory of my children in Jesus name.
10. Powers enquiring about me, receive confusion and madness in Jesus name.

WEAPON 6: THE SPIRT OF GOLIATH (1Sam 17:4, 8, 9 &16)

AND THERE WENT OUT A CHAMPION OUT OF THE CAMP OF THE PHILISTINES, NAMED GOLIATH, OF GATH, WHOSE HEIGHT WAS SIX CUBITS AND A SPAN… AND HE STOOD AND CRIED UNTO THE ARMIES OF ISRAEL, AND SAID UNTO THEM, WHY ARE YE COME OUT TO SET YOUR BATTLE IN ARRAY? AM NOT I A PHILISTINE, AND YE SERVANTS TO SAUL? CHOOSE YOU A MAN FOR YOU, AND LET HIM COME DOWN TO ME. IF HE BE ABLE TO FIGHT WITH ME, AND TO KILL ME, THEN WILL WE BE YOUR SERVANTS: BUT IF I PREVAIL AGAINST HIM, AND KILL HIM, THEN SHALL YE BE OUR SERVANTS, AND SERVE US… **AND THE PHILISTINE DREW NEAR MORNING AND EVENING, AND PRESENTED HIMSELF FORTY DAYS**".

The sixth weapon to talk about is the spirit of Goliath. Before I continue, there is something you might need to know that when we say the spirit of Herod or Goliath, it simply means there is a spirit with the character exhibited by these personalities, either Jezebel, Herod, Goliath or Pharaoh.

John the Baptist came in the spirit and power of Elijah. What you see outside is John the Baptist but the spirit and power working is that of Elijah. Likewise, for example, you may see a man called Ken, but the spirit and power working through Ken may be a strong marine or familiar spirit.

In the case of this weapon – spirit of Goliath – we will see some characteristics of the man called Goliath exhibited and you agree that there are many evil persons who behave like him. They are the ones with the spirit of Goliath.

SOME CHARACTERISTICS OF THE SPIRIT OF GOLIATH

1. It is an oppressive spirit
2. It is a stagnating spirit – "*AND THE PHILISTINE DREW NEAR MORNING AND EVENING, AND PRESENTED* ***HIMSELF FORTY DAYS***" He kept them in that position for forty days
3. It is a fearful spirit
4. It is a spirit that does not respect God
5. It is a prison, servitude spirit – "*...IF HE BE ABLE TO FIGHT WITH ME, AND TO KILL ME, THEN WILL WE BE YOUR SERVANTS: BUT IF I PREVAIL AGAINST HIM, AND KILL HIM,* ***THEN SHALL YE BE OUR SERVANTS, AND SERVE US***... " This spirit is negotiating the Israelites into slavery.
6. It's a boastful spirit. The devil is always boastful, even though if you resist him he will run. It is cowards who run when challenged
7. This spirit takes advantage of your ignorance. As long as the Israelites saw themselves as servants of Saul and not as armies of the living God they were in bondage. When David came, see what he said, "*... What shall be done to the man that killeth this Philistine, and taketh away the reproach from Israel? for who is this uncircumcised Philistine,* ***that he should defy the armies of the living God****.....Then said David to the Philistine, Thou comest to me with a sword, and with a spear, and with a shield:* ***but I come to thee in the name of the Lord of hosts, the God of the armies of Israel, whom thou hast***

defied" *(V26 & 45)* David said they were armies of the living God. Goliath said, "*… Why are ye come out to set your battle in array? am not I a Philistine, and* ***ye servants to Saul****? choose you a man for you, and let him come down to me*" (V8). He called them servants of Saul! When you don't know who you are Goliath will take advantage of you.

8. This is a very intimidating spirit. For whatever reason, the physical height was a major barrier for the children of Israel in fighting him.
9. It is a spirit with the backing of gods. He cursed David in the name of his god – Dagon.

HOW TO DEFEAT THE SPIRIT OF GOLIATH

1. You must know who you are.
2. You must have an understanding of the New Covenant – Redemption.
3. You must not allow the physical appearance of the enemy to scare you.
4. Go to battle in the name of the Lord – Ps 20.
5. You must be bold and declare your victory in the name of Jesus.
6. Understand that you belong to the armies of God not Saul.
7. In the face of opposition and envy, keep your confession of victory strong and loud. When David was disdained, he never bothered, he kept on declaring, "WHAT SHALL BE DONE TO THE MAN WHO KILLS GOLIATH….", "*… The Lord that delivered me out of*

the paw of the lion, and out of the paw of the bear, he will deliver me out of the hand of this Philistine…", "… ***Then said David to the Philistine,*** *Thou comest to me with a sword, and with a spear, and with a shield: but I come to thee in the name of the Lord* of hosts, the God of the armies of Israel, whom thou hast defied. ***This day will the Lord*** deliver thee into mine hand; and I will smite thee, and take thine head from thee; and I will give the carcases of the host of the Philistines this day unto the fowls of the air, and to the wild beasts of the earth; *that all the earth may know that there is a God in Israel. And all this assembly shall know that the Lord saveth not with sword and spear: for the battle is the Lord's, and he will give you into our hands*" **1Sam 17:26, 37 & 45-47.**

8. As far as David was concerned, Goliath was already dead. Take your lesson from that, as far as you are concerned, victory is yours.

PRAYERS AGAINST THE SPIRIT OF GOLIATH

1. Goliath intimidating me, I command you to be bound in Jesus name.
2. Every spirit of fear released against me, I take authority over you in Jesus name.
3. I cut off the head of every Goliath militating against me.
4. You spirit of Goliath assigned to paralyse my potential, I bind you in Jesus name.
5. Fire of God, consume the Goliath boasting against my God in Jesus name.
6. Any agenda by the Goliath of my environment is scattered in Jesus name.

WEAPON 7: THE SPIRT OF JEZEBEL (SEE 1KINGS 18, 19 & 21)

This is the spirit that appears not to be in charge but in the real sense it is in charge. The spirit of counterfeit spiritual authority! They are often behind the scenes, they rule from behind. Jezebel was a very strange woman in the Bible due to the atrocities she committed and made others to commit. *"But there was none like unto Ahab, which did sell himself to work wickedness in the sight of the Lord,* ***WHOM JEZEBEL HIS WIFE STIRRED UP"*** **1Kings 21:25**

Ahab had the audacity and effrontery to do evil because he married Jezebel. The person you end up with in marriage will determine what you can do or not do. There was a demonic boldness that Jezebel possessed. She transferred it to Ahab and made him do evil. Ahab without Jezebel is a nice man/king. Ahab with Jezebel is a catastrophe.

There are men who are good on their own if you take away the wife's influence, but the same men will act strangely with the influence of the wife. There was nothing Ahab wanted that he couldn't get as long as he told Jezebel, with the help of strange gods, Jezebel knew how to work her way round to get whatever she wanted by any means.

In the reign of Ahab, Jezebel was a force to reckon with, in fact, if you take a close look, she was the real king because anything she says is what Ahab the figure head does. She possessed a level of authority that is beyond normal.

JEZEBEL KILLED NABOTH

And it came to pass after these things, that Naboth the Jezreelite had a vineyard, which was in Jezreel, hard by the palace of Ahab king of Samaria. And Ahab spake unto Naboth, saying, Give me thy vineyard, that I may have it for a garden of herbs, because it is near unto my house: and I will give thee for it a better vineyard than it; or, if it seem good to thee, I will give thee the worth of it in money. And Naboth said to Ahab, The Lord forbid it me, that I should give the inheritance of my fathers unto thee. And Ahab came into his house heavy and displeased because of the word which Naboth the Jezreelite had spoken to him: for he had said, I will not give thee the inheritance of my fathers. And he laid him down upon his bed, and turned away his face, and would eat no bread. But Jezebel his wife came to him, and said unto him, why is thy spirit so sad, that thou eatest no bread". **1Kings 21:1-5**

Ahab had just seen a vineyard that he loved but belongs to someone else called Naboth. Ahab wanted it but Naboth rejected the king's offer. Coming home sad, Jezebel asked her husband why he was looking dejected and he said it was because Naboth would not give him his land. Jezebel's answer was remarkable, "*...And Jezebel his wife said unto him, Dost thou now govern the kingdom of Israel? arise, and eat bread, and let thine heart be merry:* ***I WILL GIVE THEE THE VINEYARD OF NABOTH THE JEZREELITE****". (V7)*

She said I WILL GIVE YOU THE VINEYARD OF NABOTH. Jezebel had the power to collect what doesn't belong to her and give it to whoever she wants. You need a measure of power to do that. True to her words, she organized Naboth to be killed and got the land for her husband. Let's few characteristics of this spirit:

CHARACTERISTICS OF JEZEBEL SPIRIT

1. It is against the genuine Prophetic spirit. Every prophet knows that one spirit they must deal with is the Jezebel spirit. It was Jezebel who killed all the prophets, "*For it was so,* ***WHEN JEZEBEL CUT OFF THE PROPHETS OF THE LORD...***" **1 Kings 18:4**

2. It sponsors and feeds false prophets, "*Now therefore send, and gather to me all Israel unto Mount Carmel, and the prophets of Baal four hundred and fifty, and the prophets of the groves four hundred,* ***WHICH EAT***

AT JEZEBEL'S TABLE. 1Kings 18:19. These 850 false prophets ate at Jezebel's table.

3. It has the blood of the Prophets – God's servants – on her hands. "…**THAT I MAY AVENGE THE BLOOD OF MY SERVANTS THE PROPHETS,** *and the blood of all the servants of the Lord, at the hand of Jezebel"* **2Kings 9:7**

4. It is a spirit of affluence and influence but used for the evil personal gains. To feed 850 mouths, you must have a level of wealth which often comes with a tremendous level of influence. Remember she is the king's wife. She used this to kill Naboth, *"**So she wrote letters in Ahab's name**, and sealed them with his seal…* "**1Kings 21:8.** Power drunk!

5. It is a strong demonic audacious spirit - "*Then Jezebel sent a messenger unto Elijah, saying,* **SO LET THE GODS DO TO ME, AND MORE ALSO, IF I MAKE NOT THY LIFE AS THE LIFE OF ONE OF THEM BY TOMORROW ABOUT THIS TIME". 1Kings 19:1**

6. It is a spirit that is able to put a person on the run – *"Then Jezebel sent a messenger unto Elijah, saying, So let the gods do to me, and more also, if I make not thy life as the life of one of them by tomorrow about this time. And when he saw that,* **HE AROSE, AND WENT FOR HIS LIFE,** *and came to Beersheba, which belongeth to Judah, and left his servant there"* **1Kings 19:1-2.** By what Elijah heard, he had to run for his life. How can a man kill 850 prophets of Baal and then run from a woman! That is to tell you that the spirit and power backing Jezebel is more than those behind all the 850 prophets of Baal.

7. It is a spirit that engender suicidal thought and acts in the victim – *"But he himself went a day's journey into the wilderness, and came and sat down under a juniper tree:* **AND HE REQUESTED FOR HIMSELF THAT HE MIGHT DIE***; and said, It is enough; now, O Lord, take away my life; for I am not better than my fathers"* **1Kings 19:4.** What kind of power was backing up the words Jezebel spoke that will make a prophet want to commit suicide?

8. It is a seductive spirit. There is a Church in the book of Revelation that Jesus scolded because, "*THOU SUFFEREST THAT WOMAN JEZEBEL, WHICH CALLETH HERSELF A PROPHETESS, TO TEACH* ***AND TO SEDUCE MY SERVANTS*** *TO COMMIT FORNICATION, AND TO EAT THINGS SACRIFICED UNTO IDOLS*". **Rev 2:20**

9. It is one of the spirit behind strange/false doctrines – "*THOU SUFFEREST THAT WOMAN JEZEBEL, WHICH CALLETH HERSELF A PROPHETESS,* **TO TEACH** *AND TO SEDUCE MY SERVANTS TO COMMIT FORNICATION,* **AND TO EAT THINGS SACRIFICED UNTO IDOLS". Rev 2:20.** False or wrong doctrine has the ability to destroy lives because, you see, our life ultimately goes according to what we believe and if you have imbibed a wrong doctrine, you will soon be misbehaving. Jezebel – a type of a false teacher – was seducing and teaching that eating things sacrificed to idol is not a sin.

10. It is a spirit rooted in witchcraft – "*. . . And he answered, What peace,* **SO LONG AS THE WHOREDOMS**

OF THY MOTHER JEZEBEL AND HER WITCHCRAFTS ARE SO MANY". 2Kings 9:22.

11. It is the spirit behind immorality – ***"THOU SUFFEREST THAT WOMAN JEZEBEL,*** *WHICH CALLETH HERSELF A PROPHETESS, TO TEACH AND TO* ***SEDUCE MY SERVANTS TO COMMIT FORNICATION,*** *AND TO EAT THINGS SACRIFICED UNTO IDOLS"* **Rev 2:20**. The warning went further here to say, *"and I gave her space to repent of her fornication; and she repented not. Behold,* ***I WILL CAST HER INTO A BED, AND THEM THAT COMMIT ADULTERY WITH HER INTO GREAT TRIBULATION, EXCEPT THEY REPENT OF THEIR DEEDS. AND I WILL KILL HER CHILDREN WITH DEATH;*** *and all the churches shall know that I am he which searcheth the reins and hearts…"* **Rev 2:21-23.** The Lord is jealous about the purity of the Church. Every leader in the Church should be, especially those in the five-fold ministry. When people stand to minister on the pulpit they emit spirits, "The spirit entered into me when he spake unto me…" **Ez 2:2**. If the spirit is not right, there will be strange happenings in the Church.
12. It is a very stubborn spirit that doesn't repent – *"And I gave her space to repent of her fornication;* **AND SHE REPENTED NOT" Rev 2:21.** Some people will not repent, especially when possessed with this evil spirit of Jezebel. They are bent on seeing evil upon people.
13. It is the spirit that leads astray - *"THOU SUFFEREST THAT WOMAN JEZEBEL,* ***WHICH CALLETH HERSELF A PROPHETESS, TO TEACH AND TO SEDUCE MY SERVANTS…"*** The word translated

SEDUCE is from the Greek word, "PLANAO" which means to lead astray, lead aside from the right way, wander, roam, lead into error and sin, to deceive, lead aside from the path of virtue. That means if you stay under the spirit of Jezebel, you will loose your sense of right or wrong. You will say the things that are wrong are right, and vice versa.

HOW TO OVERCOME THE SPIRIT OF JEZEBEL

1. Be strong in the Lord - **Eph 6:10-12.**
2. Be very strong in your own grace and calling – **2Tim 2:1.**
3. You need the Jehu's anointing – **2Kings 9: 1-10 & 30-37.**
4. Be strong on the right diet of the Bible doctrine – **1Tim 4:16.**

PRAYERS AGAINST THE SPIRIT OF JEZEBEL

1. I take authority over any spirit of Jezebel assigned against me in Jesus name.
2. Jezebel spirit fighting my calling I arrest you with fire in Jesus name.
3. Every spirit of seduction assigned to make me fall, be arrested in Jesus name.
4. Weapons from the marine kingdom against my ministry, catch fire in Jesus name.
5. Evil decree by any Jezebel spirit will not come to pass in my life in Jesus name.
6. Fire of God to burn, destroy and cut off every demonic prophet of Baal, overshadow my calling in Jesus name.
7. Holy Ghost, anoint me afresh to cut down the root of Jezebel troubling my calling and ministry.
8. I refuse to eat at the table of Jezebel in Jesus name.
9. Witchcraft powers behind any human being assigned to fight my calling, I arrest you in Jesus name.
10. No weapon formed against me shall prosper in Jesus name.
11. Nothing shall by any means hurt me in Jesus name.

WEAPON 8: THE ARCHERS (Gen 49: 22-24)

Joseph is a fruitful bough, even a fruitful bough by a well; whose branches run over the wall: **THE ARCHERS HAVE SORELY GRIEVED HIM, AND SHOT AT HIM, AND HATED HIM**: *But his bow abode in strength, and the arms of his hands were made strong by the hands of the mighty God of Jacob; (from thence is the shepherd, the stone of Israel).*

Here, Jacob had been blessing his children, when it came to the turn of Joseph, he made some startling statements about Joseph one of which gives us Prophetic insight into what happened to transpire between Joseph and his brothers. Jacob said it was the work of the archers. "THE ARCHERS HAVE SORELY GRIEVED HIM, AND SHOT AT HIM, AND HATED HIM…".

Joseph was grieved, that means they made him sorrowful. They shot at him because he was hated. The main reason he was sold into slavery was because of hatred. He didn't offend them! You don't have to offend the archers before they strike.

GRIEVED HIM, AND SHOT AT HIM, AND HATED HIM

Let us do a little study on Joseph to see how he provoked the archers to warrant the arrows they shot at him. I pray that any archer shooting arrows at you shall be disgraced.

The first reason was that he was very much loved by his father, "*Now Israel loved Joseph more than all his children, because he was the son of his old age: and he made him a coat of many colours.* **AND WHEN HIS BRETHREN SAW THAT THEIR FATHER LOVED HIM MORE THAN ALL HIS BRETHREN, THEY HATED HIM, AND COULD NOT SPEAK PEACEABLY UNTO HIM". Gen 37:3-4**

This was a mistake by Jacob, he opened the door for the envy and jealousy to reign in his family by showing openly the love for Joseph over his siblings. Parents, you may have your choice amongst your children but please do not show it, you may start a war that you can't end.

They all knew that Joseph was the preferred, so if you need anything from Jacob, all you need to do is send Joseph to get it. Joseph doesn't know how NO sounds, but the brothers are used to their dad's stern voice "NO". This was his first offence and why THEY HATED HIM.

The second reason was that he had a dream. Having a dream is not a problem, but telling the wrong people your dreams is a disaster. You must learn to keep your dreams to yourself or share with your fathers/mothers in the Lord. Joseph didn't learn on time so the archers rose against him.

"AND JOSEPH DREAMED A DREAM, AND HE TOLD IT TO HIS BRETHREN: AND THEY HATED HIM YET THE MORE. *And he said unto them, Hear, I pray you, this dream which I have dreamed: For, behold, we were binding sheaves in the field, and, lo, my sheaf arose, and also stood upright; and, behold, your sheaves stood round about, and made obeisance to my sheaf. And his brethren said to him, Shalt thou indeed reign over us? or shalt thou indeed have dominion over us?* **AND THEY HATED HIM YET THE MORE FOR HIS DREAMS, AND FOR HIS WORDS.** *And he dreamed yet another dream, and told it to his brethren, and said, Behold, I have dreamed a dream more; and, behold, the sun and the moon and the eleven stars made obeisance to me. And he told it to his father, and to his brethren: and his father rebuked him, and said unto him, What is this dream that thou hast dreamed? Shall I and thy mother and thy brethren indeed come to bow down ourselves to thee to the earth?* **AND HIS BRETHREN ENVIED HIM**; *but his father observed the saying".* **Gen 37:5-11**

As he was speaking the brothers were hating him as he continued, envy rose within them and finally they resorted, "*... when* *they saw him afar off, even before he came near unto them,* ***THEY CONSPIRED AGAINST HIM TO SLAY HIM.*** *And they said one to another, Behold, this dreamer cometh. Come now therefore,* ***AND LET US SLAY HIM, AND CAST HIM INTO SOME PIT,*** *and we will say, Some evil beast hath devoured him:* **AND WE SHALL SEE WHAT WILL BECOME OF HIS DREAMS**". (V18-20).

The archers are evil conspirators, they wanted him dead by all means because he had a dream. The account in Genesis 37 showed us what happened physically, but the Prophetic statement of Jacob in Genesis 49 tells us what happened in the spirit. This means an arrow can be fired into a life in the spirit and if person is without a strong Prophetic – Holy Ghost – insight, he will be battling with the wrong thing. In the spirit they GRIEVED HIM, AND SHOT AT HIM, AND HATED HIM.

They offended him, hated him AND SHOT AT HIM. But blessed be God, "*But his bow abode in strength, and the arms of his hands were made strong by the hands of the mighty God of Jacob*".

Wherever there is hatred, envy and strife like we see in the situation of Joseph, the archers will be at work doing every evil that you can imagine (See James 3:13-16). It was Paul that made this statement, "*But if ye bite and devour one another, take heed that ye be not consumed one of another*". **Gal 5:15.**

It starts with biting then moves on to devouring and the final stage is CONSUMPTION. That simply means, you will fire arrows at each other and kill one another.

CHARACTERISTICS OF ARCHERS

1. They are tactical.
2. They are focused.
3. They are thorough and diligent.
4. They have a high level concentration.

5. They have steady hands.

6. They are envious and hateful.

7. They always have a target.

INSTRUMENTS OF ARCHERS

1. Bow.

2. Arrows.

In Rick Joyner's book, The Final Quest, he made mention of something I will refer to about Bows and Arrows. He had a revelation where the enemy was attacking the Church and part of the instruments they carried were bows and arrows. He said the arrows were named Accusations, Gossip, Slander and Faultfinding. This will give us the picture of what we are talking about, though, the Bow and Arrow are physical, they have spiritual interpretation. When you slander, backbit, carry rumour, bring false accusation against someone else, it is likely the arrows representing these evils have hit you. Rick said, those who were hit by the arrows of Slander began to slander those who were not wounded, those hit by the arrows of Gossip began to gossip. In other words, you do according to the arrow that hits you

HOW TO PREVAIL AGAINST THE ARCHERS

"...But his bow abode in strength, and the arms of his hands were made strong by the hands of the mighty God of Jacob; (from thence is the shepherd, the stone of Israel Even by the God of thy father, who shall help thee; and by the Almighty, who shall bless thee with blessings of heaven above, blessings of the deep that lieth under, blessings of the breasts, and of the womb". **Gen 49:24-25**

1. Your bow – the shield of faith – must be strong – **Eph 6:16**

2. Ask the Lord to make your hands strong – **Ps 144:1 & Ps 18:34.**
3. Be strong in the Lord and in the power of His might.
4. Ask the Lord to help you – **Ps 20:1.**
5. Go for the blessings of the deep that lieth under and that of the breast and of the womb. i.e. go after those who has the anointing to righteously bless e.g. your parents both in the spirit and in the flesh, pastor or a father figure.

PRAYERS AGAINST THE ARCHERS

1. I destroy the bow and arrows of every evil archer targeting me in Jesus name.
2. I confuse the mind of every archer assigned to harm me.
3. Let blindness cover the eyes of occultic archers in Jesus name.
4. Weapons of archers, kill your owners in Jesus name.
5. Archers assigned to hurt my calling shall be disgraced in Jesus name.
6. Archers firing evil darts at me, fall down and die in Jesus name.
7. Envious and jealous spirits assigned to cast me into the pit, scatter in Jesus name.
8. Weapons of the devourers through the archers, catch fire now in Jesus name.
9. I receive strength against the arrows of the archers.
10. I hide myself in the Rock of Ages.

WEAPON 9: THE YOKE AND THE BURDEN (See Is 9:4, 10:27; 58:6 & Mat 11:30)

The ninth weapon we are looking at is a very peculiar one in that its two – YOKE AND BURDEN. They go hand in hand, most likely wherever you find one, you find another. Whenever there is a yoke, it will lead to a burden and also, wherever there is a burden, a yoke is somewhere in the hiding.

Jesus said, "*Come unto me,* **ALL YE THAT LABOUR (YOKE) AND ARE HEAVY LADEN (BURDEN)**, *and I will give you rest*" **Mat 11:28**. Jesus, by the Holy Spirit described two things that could be happening to anyone. Firstly, the person here is labouring, secondly, despite the labouring, he is heavily loaded with problems. Having been a pastor for a while now, I have had to counsel many people who are both labouring and heavily loaded with life's problems and cares.

ISSUE OF BLOOD

An example of a person shackled by yoke and loaded with burden is the woman with the issue of blood, who had been in that horrible position for many years. You find her story in throughout the gospel except for the book of John. I will give the account from the gospels of Luke and Mark. They paint a more vivid picture of the woman and her history.

Luke's account states, "*And a woman having an issue of blood twelve years, which had spent all her living upon physicians, neither could be healed of any*". **Luke 8:43**

Mark's account states, "*And a certain woman, which had an issue of blood twelve years, and had suffered many things of many physicians, and had spent all that she had, and was nothing bettered*, **BUT RATHER GREW WORSE**, *when she had heard of Jesus, came in the press behind, and touched his garment*". **Mark 5:25-27**

Now we see a clearer picture of a woman that had a yoke and a burden in her life. The yoke was that she had an issue of blood for twelve years, blood was flowing uncontrollably from her for twelve year, though the bible did not say anything about her marriage I believe that the husband would have left because that meant twelve years of no intimacy. Because of the flow, her life was restricted. She couldn't do as she would. The yoke restricts a man. Her life schedule has been disrupted by the evil flow. She had numerous hospital appointments that couldn't help her. The bible said she suffered many things from the physician – we would call a gynaecologist.

The burden on the other hand was the fact that all she had been sold and spent on this evil disease, she didn't get better. It's one thing for you to spend all your money and see results but it's frustrating when there is nothing to show for it. When men and women have nothing to show as the result of their labour in life, there will be a burden.

JESUS CURES THE ISSUE OF BLOOD

"WHEN SHE HAD HEARD OF JESUS, CAME IN THE PRESS BEHIND, AND TOUCHED HIS GARMENT. FOR SHE SAID, IF I MAY TOUCH BUT HIS CLOTHES, I SHALL BE WHOLE. AND STRAIGHTWAY THE FOUNTAIN OF HER BLOOD WAS DRIED UP; AND SHE FELT IN HER BODY THAT SHE WAS HEALED OF THAT PLAGUE. *And Jesus, immediately knowing in himself that virtue had gone out of him, turned him about in the press, and said, Who touched my clothes. And he looked round about to see her that had done this thing. But the woman fearing and trembling, knowing what was done in her, came and fell down before him, and told him all the truth. And he said unto her, Daughter, thy faith hath made thee whole; go in peace, and be whole of thy plague".* **Mark 5:27-30 & 32-34**

The yoke and the burden can be destroyed by the anointing, *"And it shall come to pass in that day, that his burden shall be taken away from off thy shoulder,* **AND HIS YOKE FROM OFF THY NECK, AND THE YOKE SHALL BE DESTROYED BECAUSE OF THE ANOINTING". Is 10:27**

Nothing else can handle this demonic weapon, experts cannot help. The woman with the issue of blood suffered from the hands of doctors, she was humiliated because the cure and freedom is not in expertise, but in the Spirit of the Lord. There are many circumstances where many have found themselves that the expert can't help them. If that is your case, go to the one that said, "*COME UNTO ME,* ALL YE THAT LABOUR AND ARE HEAVY LADEN *AND I WILL GIVE YOU REST*".

CHARACTERISTICS OF THE YOKE AND THE BURDEN

1. It stagnates.
2. It restricts.
3. It leads to depression and oppression.
4. You wouldn't be able to do as an occasion demands.
5. It may lead to you selling all you have.
6. It makes foolish the knowledge of the experts.

HOW TO DESTROY THE YOKE AND THE BURDEN

1. Engage in spiritual warfare with the weapon of:

   A. Prayer and Fasting – **Is 58:6.**

   B. The Anointing and the anointed – Jesus was anointed for the woman with the issue of blood.

2. Be determined – the woman said, "*For she said, If I may touch but his clothes, I shall be whole*" **Mark 5:28.**

3. Go to the yoke break Himself. – Jesus Christ

PRAYERS AGAINST THE YOKE AND THE BURDEN

1. I break every yoke placed upon my life in Jesus name.
2. By the anointing, let every burden upon me be lifted in Jesus name.
3. Holy ghost fire destroys the foundation of evil yoke in me.
4. Anointing that breaks the yoke overshadows my life in Jesus name.
5. Yokes and burden assigned to change my identity, catch fire in Jesus name.
6. By the finger of God, let every yoke be destroyed in Jesus name.

Chapter Three

WHY DOES THE ENEMY HURT PEOPLE?

"Therefore rejoice, ye heavens, and ye that dwell in them. Woe to the inhabiters of the earth and of the sea! ***FOR THE DEVIL IS COME DOWN UNTO YOU, HAVING GREAT WRATH, BECAUSE HE KNOWETH THAT HE HATH BUT A SHORT TIME".***

REV 12:12

It is the job of the enemy – Devil – to attack people. He may use different persons, circumstances and situations to do it but it has to be done. He knows he has a short time.

Many times I hear people say to me, "why me?" "Why is this attack increasing"? I laugh, and my reply is often that the devil is doing his job, you too do your job. I realise that when there is nothing putting some people on the run, they don't take spiritual activities such as prayer, fasting and reading the word seriously. It is when the devil has risen against them, that is when they rise up too. That means if the devil does not do his job, you probably wouldn't do what you are meant to do to stay spiritually fit.

A sister told of some terrible dreams she had been having and was complaining that it was too much. She said the devil is focusing on her and that she didn't collect anything from him. I told her you don't have to collect anything from him. The devil is the devil and his job is to do evil by whatever means possible. He may do that by appearing in your dreams – which was what he did in the case of this particular sister – or he may use other methods. Your concern is not the methods; your concern is to be armed with adequate weapons needed to defeat him.

SCRIPTURAL BACKGROUND TO THE ENMITY BETWEEN MAN AND DEVIL

Let us now see the reason why the devil hurts people. We will not understand why until we know the background about him and where he was before. We have a perfect account of both his – devil's – background and one of the major reasons why he attacks people. We see it in the book of Revelation Chapter 12, "**AND WAR BROKE OUT IN HEAVEN, MICHAEL [THE ARCHANGEL] AND HIS ANGELS WAGING WAR WITH THE DRAGON. THE DRAGON AND HIS ANGELS FOUGHT, BUT THEY WERE NOT STRONG ENOUGH AND DID NOT PREVAIL, AND THERE WAS NO LONGER A PLACE FOUND FOR THEM IN HEAVEN. AND THE GREAT DRAGON WAS THROWN DOWN, THE AGE-OLD SERPENT WHO IS CALLED THE DEVIL AND SATAN, HE WHO CONTINUALLY DECEIVES AND SEDUCES THE ENTIRE INHABITED WORLD; HE WAS THROWN DOWN TO THE EARTH**, *and his angels were thrown down with him. Then I heard a loud voice in heaven, saying, "Now the salvation, and the power, and the kingdom (dominion, reign) of our God, and the authority of His Christ have come; for the accuser of our [believing] brothers and sisters has been thrown down [at last], he who accuses them and keeps bringing charges [of sinful behavior] against them before our God day and night.And they overcame and conquered him because of the blood of the Lamb and because of the word of their testimony, for they did not love their life and renounce their faith even when faced with death. Therefore rejoice, O heavens and you who dwell in them* *[in the presence of God].* **WOE TO THE EARTH AND THE SEA, BECAUSE THE DEVIL HAS COME DOWN TO YOU IN GREAT WRATH, KNOWING THAT HE HAS ONLY A SHORT TIME [REMAINING]!" AND WHEN THE DRAGON SAW THAT HE WAS THROWN DOWN TO THE EARTH, HE PERSECUTED THE WOMAN WHO HAD GIVEN BIRTH TO THE MALE CHILD.** *But the two wings of the great eagle were given to the woman, so that she could fly into the wilderness to her place, where she was nourished for a time and times and half a time (three and one-half years), away from the presence of the serpent (Satan). And the serpent hurled water like a river out of his mouth after the woman, so that he might cause her to be swept away with the flood. But the earth helped the woman, and the earth opened its mouth and swallowed up the river which the dragon had hurled out of his mouth.***SO THE DRAGON WAS ENRAGED WITH THE WOMAN, AND HE WENT OFF TO WAGE WAR ON THE REST OF HER CHILDREN (SEED), THOSE WHO KEEP AND OBEY THE COMMANDMENTS OF GOD AND HAVE THE TESTIMONY OF JESUS [HOLDING FIRMLY TO IT AND BEARING WITNESS TO HIM]. Rev 12:7-17AMP.** (See Gen 3:15).

Somehow, the devil thought he could also be like God and receive all the glory, majesty and honour that he saw other angels give to God. (See Isaiah 14 and Ezekiel 28)

He put up a fight in the heaven and lost. He was cast down. This was what Jesus referred to before he said, behold I give unto you power. He had said, "...I BEHELD SATAN AS LIGHTNING FALL FROM HEAVEN" **Luke 10:18.** Jesus said I was there when the great dragon, old serpent, devil, Satan and the deceiver was cast down to the earth with his angels, it was as though lightning fell. It will be good to note that it wasn't only the Devil that was cast down to the earth, his angels were also cast out of heaven. These are the fallen angels. The Bible referred to those angels as, "...HIS ANGELS....".

The devil's angel. These are the angels he was able to convince into rebelling against God and some of those angels were originally under his command as Lucifer the Archangel.

Having been cast out of heaven into the earth and also knowing where he will end and that his judgement will be soon, he got mad and declared war against humanity. The Bible says the Devil is come down, "...*UNTO YOU, HAVING GREAT WRATH, BECAUSE HE KNOWETH THAT HE HATH BUT A SHORT TIME*". He has come down UNTO YOU! Not onto them, we, us or they BUT UNTO YOU! Personal Satanic encounters against everyone. As long as you are an inhabiter of the earth, the Bible says, "WOE UNTO YOU..." Why? "FOR THE DEVIL IS COME DOWN UNTO YOU".

The Bible went further to say, "*AND WHEN THE DRAGON SAW THAT HE WAS CAST UNTO THE EARTH, HE PERSECUTED THE WOMAN WHICH BROUGHT FORTH THE MAN CHILD*" v13. When he saw that there had been a change of residence, he unleashed terror on the whole world.

Finally, "...*THE DRAGON WAS ENRAGED WITH THE WOMAN,* ***AND HE WENT OFF TO WAGE WAR ON THE REST OF HER CHILDREN (SEED)****, THOSE WHO KEEP AND OBEY THE COMMANDMENTS OF GOD AND HAVE THE TESTIMONY OF JESUS [HOLDING FIRMLY TO IT AND BEARING WITNESS TO HIM]*". In this verse, we see that the devil will make war against anyone who keeps and obeys the commandments of God and those who have the testimony of Jesus Christ. If this is you, be ready for war!

In conclusion, the Devil hurt people because –

1. That is his job.
2. There is a change in his residence – from heaven to the earth. He makes war on all the inhabitants of the earth and of the sea.

3. You keep the commandments of God.
4. You obey the commandments of God.
5. You have the testimony of Jesus.

If you don't want the Devil to attack you, do the following –

1. Don't keep and obey the commandments of God.
2. Don't have the testimony of Jesus.
3. Don't live on the earth, find another planet!

If these three are not possible for you, then get ready for a fight. We have the victory through the blood of the lamb. "AND THEY OVERCAME HIM – THE DEVIL – BY THE BLOOD OF THE LAMB AND BY THE WORD OF THEIR TESTIMONY…". **Rev 12:11**

Behold, I give unto you power to tread on serpents and scorpions, and over all the power of the enemy: and
NOTHING SHALL BY ANY MEANS HURT YOU.
Luke 10:19

Chapter Four

WHEN DOES THE ENEMY HURT PEOPLE?

*"**BUT WHILE MEN SLEPT**, HIS ENEMY CAME AND SOWED TARES AMONG THE WHEAT, AND WENT HIS WAY. BUT WHEN THE BLADE WAS SPRUNG UP, AND BROUGHT FORTH FRUIT, THEN APPEARED THE TARES ALSO. SO THE SERVANTS OF THE HOUSEHOLDER CAME AND SAID UNTO HIM, SIR, DIDST NOT THOU SOW GOOD SEED IN THY FIELD? FROM WHENCE THEN HATH IT TARES? HE SAID UNTO THEM, AN ENEMY HATH DONE THIS..."*

Mat 13:25-28

Our Lord Jesus gave a parable, in this chapter we will be looking closely at that parable to learn few things.

Jesus said a man sowed good seed in his field BUT WHILST HE SLEPT something happened, the enemy came in and hurt him by SOWING TARES AMONGST THE WHEAT.

The wheat is the good, blessing and testimony but the tares are the problems, calamity and ill-luck.

This shows that when an individual is asleep, the enemy can hurt him. The sleep Jesus speaks of here is not only talking of physical sleep but also a state of spiritual dullness, laxity and lukewarmness. The word translated "SLEPT" is from the Greek word "*KATHEUDO*" which means, drop off to sleep, to lie down, to yield to sloth and sin, to be indifferent, to lie down to rest.

Did you notice that as soon as the evil seed – tares – was sown the ENEMY WENT HIS WAY. Meaning, devils don't waste time. They know their duties and go to do it. The kingdom of darkness is a highly-organised kingdom, you can't defeat him if you are not organized.

THE BLADE AND TARES

Jesus mentioned something here, he said, "...BUT WHEN THE BLADE WAS SPRUNG UP, AND BROUGHT FORTH FRUIT, THEN APPEARED THE TARES ALSO...".

Two things are now happening together – the bad and the good. The blessings and the misfortune. When the blade came up with fruit, then the evil seed also came up with tares. This is when you have the good and bad happening at the same time. Marriage and career is great, but health is in shambles.

KNOW YOUR FIELD AND KNOW YOUR ENEMY

Another lesson from this is that the man that owned this field knew what he planted. The servant said, "THE SERVANTS OF THE HOUSEHOLDER CAME AND SAID UNTO HIM, **SIR, DIDST NOT THOU SOW GOOD SEED IN THY FIELD?** FROM WHENCE THEN HATH IT TARES? HE SAID UNTO THEM, AN ENEMY HATH DONE THIS...".

He knew what he planted in his field, so when what should not be growing began to grow he knew that the power of darkness was at work. He knew an enemy had been around.

The reason why some people are not fighting is because they don't know their field, they don't know what to expect. If you work in an organisation, you expect to be paid a salary. If you don't receive the salary you will at some point ask questions, either from the boss or HR. You did that because you knew your field and what to expect.

Many are down in life and are not asking question because they don't know their field.

It is not enough to know your field – what you have invested and what you are expecting – you must also know your enemy. When the master was questioned by the servant, "*SIR, DIDST NOT THOU SOW GOOD SEED IN THY FIELD? FROM WHENCE THEN HATH IT TARES*" the master answered, "**AN ENEMY HATH DONE THIS…**". When you know your enemy, you know what he can do and you will be able to plan ahead.

This man didn't say let me go and pray, he had enough knowledge to be able to spot the works of darkness. There are those who are in the midst of evil works and activities but can't discern. If you can't discern your enemy, you can't win any battle. You won't know what to do to get victory.

THE TWO HARLOTS

"*Then came there two women, that were harlots, unto the king, and stood before him. And the one woman said, O my lord, I and this woman dwell in one house; and* **I WAS DELIVERED OF A CHILD WITH HER IN THE HOUSE.** *And it came to pass the third day after that I was delivered, that this woman was delivered also: and we were together; there was no stranger with us in the house, save we two in the house.* **AND THIS WOMAN'S CHILD DIED IN THE NIGHT; BECAUSE SHE OVERLAID IT. AND SHE AROSE AT MIDNIGHT, AND TOOK MY SON FROM BESIDE ME, WHILE THINE HANDMAID SLEPT, AND LAID IT IN HER BOSOM, AND LAID HER DEAD CHILD IN MY BOSOM. AND WHEN I ROSE IN THE MORNING TO GIVE MY CHILD SUCK, BEHOLD, IT WAS DEAD: BUT WHEN I HAD CONSIDERED IT IN THE MORNING, BEHOLD, IT WAS NOT MY SON, WHICH I DID BEAR.** *And the other woman said, Nay; but the living is my son, and the dead is thy son. And this said, No; but the dead is thy son, and the living is my son. Thus they spake before the king. Then* *said the king, The one saith, This is my son that liveth, and thy son is the dead: and the other saith, Nay; but thy son is the dead, and my son is the living".* **1Kings 3:16-23**

Another incident that we will look at is recorded in the books of First Kings, Chapter 3. Solomon had just been anointed with wisdom by God in a dream and to really test or affirm that gift a situation arose.

Beyond the testing and affirmation of this gift of wisdom, what I want you to see is the thought we are dealing with in this chapter which is WHEN does the enemy hurt people? What season, what time or hour? The scripture is clear on this and that is why the story of these harlots is so essential.

Looking closely, what happened was that harlot "A" had a baby boy on Monday, and after three days, which will be Thursday, harlot "B" had a baby boy also, then a night came. Harlot "B" made a terrible mistake, her baby "**DIED IN THE NIGHT; BECAUSE SHE OVERLAID IT".** The attack on harlot B came in the night. She slept on her son. What kind of sleep will catch a mother to sleep over the son she carried for nine months? That also is a work of darkness. Harlot "B" had killed her own child by herself – she would have been charged for manslaughter if it were these days.

However, a harlot will always be a harlot. She – harlot "B" – played a fast move on harlot "A" whose son was still alive by swapping the babies. Harlot "A" was fast asleep in the night, though with a living son, but harlot "B" woke up and did what is called a satanic exchange. Harlot "B" exchanged her dead son for the son of harlot "A". The Bible says, "*AND THIS WOMAN'S CHILD DIED IN THE NIGHT; BECAUSE SHE OVERLAID IT. AND SHE (Harlot B) AROSE AT MIDNIGHT, AND TOOK MY (Harlot A) SON FROM BESIDE ME, WHILE THINE HANDMAID SLEPT,* **AND LAID IT IN HER BOSOM, AND LAID HER DEAD CHILD IN MY BOSOM**. *AND WHEN I ROSE IN THE MORNING TO GIVE MY CHILD SUCK, BEHOLD, IT WAS DEAD".*

SATANIC EXCHANGE

At night, harlot "B" laid a dead child in the bosom of harlot "A" while she slept. This is the time the enemy likes to attack – WHEN PEOPLE ARE SLEEPING!

An evil exchange happened that saw her wake up with a dead child. But thank God, harlot "A" knew what to do. She went to the king who solved the problem and she got her living baby back.

But the wisdom and lesson is this, there are those who sleep with a living child and wake up with a dead child. Some sleep with healthy bodies but wake up with a diseased body, some sleep with their glory intact but wake up with empty glory. There are those who are okay before they sleep but at night whilst they sleep the enemy comes and does an exchange. There are good marriages that at night something evil was either planted or a manipulation carried out. So, the spouse that used to be loving and caring is now spiteful. IF YOU DON'T KNOW HOW TO HANDLE YOUR NIGHT YOU WILL PAY FOR IT WITH YOUR DAY.

A man of God told a story of how his step-mother gave his glory to a step-brother. The step-brother became a manager of a company while he was a labourer in the farm, but after much prayer, power changed hands. The former labourer is now the one feeding the former manager and sending the children of the former manager to school.

If you must avoid satanic exchange, stay awake spiritually, don't be lukewarm, don't be lazy. Rise up and fight! Harlot "A" would have easily avoided that evil exchange if she didn't sleep too deep. The Bible says, *"Slothfulness casteth into a deep sleep... "*. **Prov 19:15**

When God gives you a blessing, you must know how to keep and secure that which you have. Children are the heritage of the Lord, so it was the Lord who gave harlot "A" the baby boy, but she was not strong enough to stop harlot "B" from doing the exchange. It is obvious that harlot "B" was more crooked than "A" because of the ability to make a fast move. If you must arrest satanic exchange you must be a fast thinker and see ahead.

If you read further, harlot "B", knowing fully well that the baby is not her own, still fought to hold on to the baby and when the king decided to kill the baby to see who the real mother was, harlot "B" didn't mind the baby dying. The enemy is ready to go the extra mile so as to see their evil desire come to pass. If you must prevail, you must be ready to walk in the realm of power. Naboth as we saw in the previous chapter, died and lost his inheritance – vineyard – to a witch known as Jezebel because he lacked adequate power to keep his possession.

Behold, I give unto you power to tread on serpents and scorpions,
and over all the power of the enemy: and
NOTHING SHALL BY ANY MEANS HURT YOU.
LUKE 10:19

Chapter Five

WHAT TO DO TO AVOID GETTING HURT BY THE ENEMY?

***"BEHOLD, I GIVE UNTO YOU POWER TO TREAD ON SERPENTS AND SCORPIONS, AND OVER ALL THE POWER OF THE ENEMY:** and nothing shall by any means hurt you."*
Luke 10:19

Make no mistake, THE ENEMY HAS POWER! Jesus said, I gave you power OVER ALL THE POWER OF THE ENEMY. The power we have, given to us by the head of the Church – Jesus Christ – is the power that is greater than the power of the enemy.

There are those who don't believe that the enemy has power. I am not saying this to scare you, but you must know the truth about the enemy. There are those who don't believe in devils. There are those who attribute everything wrong to devils and there are some of us who know where to place him!

If you don't know where to place the enemy, he may outwit you. Victory and deliverance starts from the day we know what we must know about the enemy and agree to it, believe it and also act on it. You will be pitied if you have imbibed the false doctrine that says Satan has no power and you can do what you like when you like.

Those who can put the devil where to belong are men of power and authority, who have known his tricks.

PRACTICAL STEPS TO TAKE

We must understand that there are weapons that God has given to His own children. The scriptures says that, "*For though we walk in the flesh,* **WE DO NOT WAR AFTER THE FLESH: (FOR THE WEAPONS OF OUR WARFARE** *are not carnal, but mighty through God to the pulling down of strong holds). Casting down imaginations, and every high thing that exalteth itself against the knowledge of God, and bringing into captivity every thought to the obedience of Christ; And having in a readiness to revenge all disobedience, when your obedience is fulfilled*". **2Cor 10:3-6**

We are walking in the flesh, but not WARRING after the flesh means, there is a fight, battle or warfare but the fight is not with the flesh. We are not fighting flesh and blood – human beings. Though the devil may work through them. Daddy Areogun said we fight the devil in three ways, firstly, in human beings, secondly, in the spirit and thirdly, in government laws. (See Matthew 4, Ephessians 6:12 & Daniel 3)

We have established 4 things –

1. We are in a state of warfare.
2. The warfare is not with flesh and blood but with spirits.
3. We have weapons.
4. The weapons are mighty.

Apostle Paul, whilst writing to the Corinthian Church, scratched the surface of the subject of this spiritual warfare but when he wrote to the Church at Ephesus, he went very deep. He repeated that there is a fight against the devil. He showed us the weapons that we have in our spiritual arsenal that can be used to defeat the devil and he also mentioned the hierarchy of the kingdom of darkness. Paul writes, "Finally, my brethren, be strong in the Lord, and in the power of his might. *Put on the whole armour of God, that ye may be able to stand against the wiles of the devil.* **FOR WE WRESTLE NOT AGAINST FLESH AND BLOOD, BUT AGAINST PRINCIPALITIES, AGAINST POWERS, AGAINST THE RULERS OF THE DARKNESS OF THIS WORLD, AGAINST SPIRITUAL WICKEDNESS IN HIGH PLACES**. *Wherefore take unto you the whole armour of God, that ye may be able to withstand in the evil day, and having done all, to stand. Stand therefore, having your loins girt about with truth, and having on the breastplate of righteousness; And your feet shod with the preparation of the gospel of peace; Above all, taking the shield of faith, wherewith ye shall be able to quench all the fiery darts of the wicked. And take the helmet of salvation, and the sword of the Spirit, which is the word of God: Praying always with all prayer and supplication in the Spirit, and watching thereunto with all perseverance and supplication for all saints*". **Eph 6:10-18**

Paul had said to the Corinthian Church that, "*for though we walk in the flesh, we do not war after the flesh***:** *the weapons of our warfare are not carnal, but mighty through God to the* **PULLING DOWN OF STRONG HOLDS**… ". He said to the Church at Ephesus what I believe the strongholds were because you could see that Paul is on the same line of thought – SPIRITUAL WARFARE. So he said, "*for we wrestle not against flesh and blood, but* **AGAINST PRINCIPALITIES, AGAINST POWERS, AGAINST THE RULERS OF THE DARKNESS OF THIS WORLD, AGAINST SPIRITUAL WICKEDNESS IN HIGH PLACES".**

HIERARCHY OF SATANIC KINGDOM DESCRIBED BY PAUL, BEGINNING WITH THE LEAST.

1. Principalities.
2. Powers.

3. Rulers of the darkness of this world.

4. Spiritual wickedness in high places.

These are the four major satanic kingdoms that every believer has to combat with, in one way or the other and at some points or seasons in our life.

After Paul had mentioned the four satanic kingdoms, he used the word, "WHEREFORE" which is an adverb and a conjunction. The meaning is "AS A RESULT OF WHICH" or "FOR THIS REASON". This is what the Apostle is simply saying, "Now that you have these four strongholds, for that reason or as a result of the nature of the warfare, take the whole armour of God. He now went further to give the whole armour, "**WHEREFORE – FOR THIS REASON** – *take unto you the whole armour of God, that ye may be able to withstand in the evil day, and having done all, to stand. Stand therefore, having your loins girt about with truth, and having on the breastplate of righteousness; And your feet shod with the preparation of the gospel of peace; Above all, taking the shield of faith, wherewith ye shall be able to quench all the fiery darts of the wicked. And take the helmet of salvation, and the sword of the Spirit, which is the word of God: Praying always with all prayer and supplication in the Spirit, and watching thereunto with all perseverance and supplication for all saints*".

THE AMOUR OF GOD – Believers weapon for warfare against the enemy. The purpose of this is, "*that ye may be able to **withstand** in the evil day, and having done all, **to stand***". Two purposes the weapons will serve – firstly, is to WITHSTAND the enemy in the evil day, meaning you remain undamaged, unaffected and able to successfully resist the enemy without any injury. Secondly, is to STAND. To withstand is different from to stand. To stand here means you are still on your feet after the battle. You are not asking to take a rest. When you watch wrestling or boxing, someone might be pronounced the winner and given the belt but might not be able to stand on his feet afterwards. He might need medical attention though he was the winner. God wants us to stand, not rushing to Accident and Emergency in the spirit after the battle. Now, let's outline the weapons God has given us:

1. Truth.
2. Righteousness.
3. Preparation of the gospel of peace.
4. Shield of faith.
5. Helmet of salvation.
6. Sword of the Spirit – the word of God.
7. Praying always in the Spirit.
8. Watching with all perseverance and supplication for all saints – Intercession.

TAKE UNTO YOU…

Paul told us what to do with these weapons in other words to maximise their use. It is one thing to have a weapon. It is entirely different when you know how to use it and also know what it can or cannot do. Paul said, "… **TAKE UNTO YOU** *the whole armour of God…* ". The Amplified version says, "**PUT ON** *the complete armour of God, so that you will be able to [successfully] resist and stand your ground in the evil day [of danger], and having done everything [that the crisis demands], to stand firm [in your place, fully prepared, immovable, victorious]*".

The New International Version (NIV) and New Living Translation (NLT) also says PUT ON. Now, either TAKE UNTO YOU or PUT ON, they both speak of an active position not a passive one. It speaks of something that must be on us all the time, wherever you are you must have all these eight weapons on.

HOW TO TAKE UNTO or HOW TO PUT ON?

The question now is how does one TAKE UNTO or PUT ON? This is very easy and simple. How do you PUT ON your clothes? You know what your clothes looks like and you just go and put your clothes on. I will give five major practical steps:

1. Know your weapons.
2. Identify your weapons.
3. Know how it works and what they really mean. Don't guess about any of the weapons. Find out through research.
4. Then wear it! This means, you DO IT. For example, how to PUT ON the weapon of truth. You just SAY THE TRUTH and DO WHAT IS TRUE! It is as simple as that. When you do that, you have PUT ON truth.
5. Use your mouth in the proper direction.

BEHOLD I GIVE UNTO YOU POWER

The other thing we must all possess apart from putting on the whole armour of God is to be empowered by the Spirit. Without this, the enemy will work unhindered and unchallenged. He will steal, kill and destroy. The Psalmist understood the need for power when he said, "*Say unto God, How terrible art thou in thy works!* **THROUGH THE GREATNESS OF THY POWER SHALL THINE ENEMIES SUBMIT THEMSELVES UNTO THEE". Ps 66:3**

The enemy will only submit themselves when they see great power in manifestation. Jesus said unto the seventy that came back rejoicing, "BEHOLD I GIVE UNTO POWER……" without this the demons wouldn't have been subject unto them. Jesus had to empower them. He gave them that which is needed to put the devils where they belong.

Jesus said to his disciples, **"...BUT TARRY YE IN THE CITY OF**

JERUSALEM, UNTIL YE BE ENDUED WITH POWER FROM ON HIGH." Luke 24:49. He said to them to wait in Jerusalem UNTIL! Until what? UNTIL YOU ARE ENDUED WITH POWER! Because without the power the devil will kill and eat them for lunch.

You see, it takes power to avoid been hurt by the enemy, Solomon said, "*So I returned, and considered all the oppressions that are done under the sun: and behold the tears of such as were oppressed, and they had no comforter; and on the side of their oppressors there was power; but they had no comforter*". **Ecc 4:1.**

SOLOMON CONSIDERED THE FOLLOWING:

1. All the oppression on the earth – he had a supernatural insight to the problems of mankind.
2. He saw the tears of the oppressed.
3. The oppressed had no comforter – i.e. they had no power. In the New Testament, the Holy Spirit is our comforter and his major work is to empower the believer.
4. The oppressor had enough power to oppress – this means, you will always be oppressed by what is more powerful than you.

A FEW THINGS TO NOTE FROM THE FINDINGS OF SOLOMON:

1. Tears will continue without power.
2. Power is not what you need but ADEQUATE AND COMMENSURATE POWER for the battle at hand.
3. You will always be oppressed by what is more powerful than you.
4. There is oppression going on under the sun.

5. If you don't want to cry, you need the Holy Spirit – THE COMFORTER.
6. The comforter is the one that can put an end to all tears.
7. There are two sides in life – The oppressed and the oppressor.
8. You are either free or you are being oppressed.
9. The enemy does not need your permission to oppress you.
10. You will automatically be oppressed if you lack power.
11. The oppressor knows if you have power or not.

There is another scripture that tells us the importance of power, "*How God anointed Jesus of Nazareth with the* **HOLY GHOST AND WITH POWER: WHO WENT ABOUT DOING GOOD, AND HEALING ALL THAT WERE OPPRESSED OF THE DEVIL**; *for God was with him*". **Acts 10:38**

FEW LESSONS FROM ACTS 10:38:

1. You don't only need the Holy Ghost, you need the power dimension of Him also.
2. It is God who anoints not man.
3. Nothing significant happens without the anointing – with Holy Ghost and Power.
4. Without the Holy Ghost and power, you can't do good.
5. Without the Holy Ghost and power, you cannot heal the oppressed.
6. The devil is behind oppression.
7. The devil is behind many sickness and diseases.

8. You need divine presence to destroy the works of darkness.

Another scripture I will like us to see and learn from is Acts Chapter one, verse eight, it reads, "*But ye shall receive power, after that the Holy Ghost is come upon you: and ye shall be witnesses unto me both in Jerusalem, and in all Judaea, and in Samaria, and unto the uttermost part of the earth*".

A FEW LESSONS FROM ACTS 1:8:

1. What you are able to do is determined by the power you possess.
2. Without the Holy Ghost, there is no power. – **Micah 3:8**
3. If you want power, go after the Holy Ghost.
4. The extent of the effect of your life, ministry, calling, business is largely dependent on the level of the Holy Ghost power baptism you possess.
5. No power no glory. – Ps 63:2
6. If you must go from Jerusalem to Judaea, Samaria and THE UTTERMOST PART OF THE EARTH you need power. i.e. If you will be all that God ordained you to be, you need power.
7. You will be limited to Jerusalem and not smell THE UTTERMOST PART OF THE EARTH when you lack the required power.

JOURNEY INTO POWER

Here we will see what to do to be empowered by the Holy Ghost. The perfect person to consider and learn from is our Lord Jesus Christ Himself. "*And Jesus being full of the Holy Ghost returned from*

Jordan, and was led by the Spirit into the wilderness. Being forty days tempted of the devil. **AND IN THOSE DAYS, HE DID EAT NOTHING**: *and when they were ended, he afterward hungered…".* **Luke 4:1-2**

Jesus had embarked on a journey into power and we see that he didn't eat anything for forty days. Afterwards, the devil came and tempted him. He passed the test and the bible recorded that, "…***JESUS RETURNED IN THE POWER OF THE SPIRIT INTO GALILEE: AND THERE WENT OUT A FAME OF HIM THROUGH ALL THE REGION ROUND ABOUT.*** *And he taught in their synagogues, being glorified of all…".* **Luke 14:14-15**. When he came out of the wilderness and had defeated the traps of the enemy, he came out a different person. What did Jesus do in the wilderness? He fasted and prayed! These two practical activities do not leave you the same. The power of the Spirit is experienced when you fast and pray often, from the time he came out of the wilderness until he was crucified. Anywhere demons saw him they bowed and worshipped him.

On the same day, he went into the synagogue to read, "*And there was delivered unto him the book of the prophet Esaias. And when he had opened the book, he found the place where it was written* **THE SPIRIT OF THE LORD IS UPON ME, BECAUSE HE HATH ANOINTED ME TO PREACH THE GOSPEL TO THE POOR; HE HATH SENT ME TO HEAL THE BROKENHEARTED, TO PREACH DELIVERANCE TO THE CAPTIVES, AND RECOVERING OF SIGHT TO THE BLIND, TO SET AT LIBERTY THEM THAT ARE BRUISED, TO PREACH THE ACCEPTABLE YEAR OF THE LORD.** *And he closed the book, and he gave it again to the minister, and sat down. And the eyes of all them that were in the synagogue were fastened on him. And he began to say unto them, This day is this scripture fulfilled in your ears*". **Luke 14:17-21**

Jesus said the Holy Ghost and Power he had received will enable him do the following:

1. Preach the gospel.
2. Heal the broken-hearted.
3. Preach and do deliverance to the captives (to those hurt by the enemy). It is one thing to preach deliverance, it is another thing to demonstrate, show and do it.
4. To recover sight to the blind.
5. To set at liberty those who are bruised.
6. Preach the acceptable year of the Lord – Year of freedom from debt and slavery. (**Lev 25:8-10**)

Because Jesus had engaged in prayer and fasting, he received the power of the Spirit to do all that we highlighted. Prayer and fasting cannot be over emphasized **IF WE ARE IN A POSITION** where the devils runs from us. A place where we can't be hurt, the demon said, "*. . . Jesus I know, and Paul I know;* **BUT WHO ARE YE". Acts 19:15.** If you don't want circumstances, situations and devils asking WHO ARE YOU, it is wise to run into the power of God.

The Apostle had met with a situation they couldn't handle but Jesus bailed them out, later, when they were alone with Jesus, they asked a serious question, "***Then came the disciples to Jesus apart, and said, Why could not we cast him out?*** **AND JESUS SAID UNTO THEM, BECAUSE OF YOUR UNBELIEF**: *for verily I say unto you, If ye have faith as a grain of mustard seed, ye shall say unto this mountain, Remove hence to yonder place; and it shall remove; and nothing shall be impossible unto you.* **HOWBEIT THIS KIND NOT OUT BUT BY PRAYER AND FASTING. Mat 17:19-21**

The three main reasons why the disciples couldn't cast out the demon:

1. Presence of unbelief.
2. Lack of adequate prayer.

3. Lack of fasting.

Jesus pointed out to them their failure in prayer and fasting was the root cause of their inability to cast out the demon. That answer shows that prayer and fasting is indispensable! If situations must change and bow, if you don't want the enemy to hurt you, you must pray and fast. This is the key!

WHEN POWER COMES, STRENGTH COMES

Power is needed to defeat the enemy. We know there is power when there is strength. When strength is displayed, power is available. Solomon said in the book of Proverbs, *"If thou faint in the day of adversity,* **THY STRENGTH IS SMALL". Prov 24:10.** When battles are lost, it is not necessarily the lack or absence of strength but the lack of ADEQUATE STRENGTH. That was why Paul said BE STRONG IN THE LORD AND IN THE POWER OF HIS MIGHT. He prayed for the Church at Ephesus that God, "*...would grant you, according to the riches of his glory,* **TO BE STRENGTHENED WITH MIGHT BY HIS SPIRIT IN THE INNER MAN". Eph 3:16.** He went further to say, *"Now unto him that is able to do exceeding abundantly above all that we ask or think,* **ACCORDING TO THE POWER THAT WORKETH IN US". Eph 3:20.** Paul says here that God can do the following:

1. Exceedingly above what we ask or think.
2. Abundantly above what we ask or think.
3. All that we ask.

But he put a clause, ACCORDING TO THE POWER THAT IS AT WORK IN US. What is available and possible is determined by the power at work in you. John said, *"I have written unto you, fathers, because ye have known him that is from the beginning.* **I HAVE WRITTEN UNTO YOU, YOUNG MEN, BECAUSE YE ARE**

STRONG, AND THE WORD OF GOD ABIDETH IN YOU, AND YE HAVE OVERCOME THE WICKED ONE". 1John 2:14

To break down what John was saying:

1. I write to you young men because you are strong. – **Prov 20:29**
2. You have the Word of God in you which produced the strength.
3. By the strength produced by the word of God, you have been able to overcome the wicked one. You can't overcome the wicked one without strength and John said the Word of God produces that strength. Jesus defeated the Devil by saying IT IS WRITTEN! The Devil can't write you off when you know what is written in the Word of God.

PRAYER FOR SALVATION

Except a man is born again he will never and can never see the kingdom of God. Salvation is mandatory for anyone that desires to enter into the kingdom of God. Without salvation no man will see God. You need to be saved from the wrath of God that is coming upon this disobedient generation. Now say this prayer……

> *Heavenly father, I come to You in the name of Your Son Jesus. Your word says that, "And it shall come to pass, that whosoever shall call on the name of the Lord be saved".* ***Act 2:21****. I am calling on you now. I pray and desire that you come into my heart now and be my Lord and Saviour according to your word which says, "That if thou shalt confess with thy mouth the Lord Jesus, and shalt believe in thine heart that God hath raised him from the dead, thou shalt be saved. For with the heart man believeth unto righteousness; and with the mouth confession is made unto salvation".* ***Romans 10:9-10****. I do that now, I believe in my heart that Jesus Christ died for me and was raised from the dead on the third day. I confess with my mouth that he is Lord. I ask that you forgive me of my sins and cleanse me with your blood. This I ask for in Jesus name. Amen*

We believe you have been saved. Look for a bible believing and teaching church that will enhance your growth in the knowledge and grace of God.

PRAYER FOR THE BAPTISM IN THE HOLY GHOST

Power is needed to run the race which you have just begun. Jesus Christ told His disciples never to go out and do anything until they have been endued with power from on high.

The power is made available by the ministry of the Holy Spirit which with an evidence of speaking in tongues. God desires that you should be baptized and speak in the heavenly language. He gives you the utterance but you will have to open your mouth and speak out boldly those words as you are given utterance.

You do not have to understand what the words means just say it out as you receive it. Say this prayer with all genuineness of heart.

> *Father Lord, I come to you in the name of Jesus Christ and I ask you to fill me with the Holy Spirit now with the evidence of speaking with tongues, because you said in your word that, "...If ye then, being evil, know how to give good gifts unto your children: how* ***much more*** *shall your* ***heavenly Father give*** *the* ***Holy Spirit to them that ask him****....".* ***Luke 11:13****. I also know from your word that, "...****everyone*** *who asks receives, and he who seeks finds, and to him who knocks it will be opened...".* **Mathew 7:8NKJV**. *Holy Spirit rise up within me now as I begin to praise God. I am ready and fully expect to speak in tongues now as You give me utterance in the name of Jesus Christ. Amen.*
>
> *Now lift up your hands and begin to praise God then speak those words as they come to you now in Jesus name. Amen*

Having received the baptism of the Holy Ghost with the evidence of speaking with tongues you must constantly speak those words.

ABOUT THE BOOK

From the well known scripture, **Luke 10:19**, the Holy Spirit has given Ayodeji a timely revelation that will benefit the body of Christ. In this book, the how, when and why of satanic attack is unveiled. You will also learn what every child of God must do to be placed in a position of power and authority over all the hosts and works of darkness.

ABOUT THE AUTHOR

Ayodeji D. Olusanmi is a teacher and a preacher of the gospel. A dynamic pastor of a branch of Mountain of Fire and Miracle Ministries - United Kingdom. He studied in the UK as a Biomedical Scientist. He is the author of *The Prayer that Works, The Testimony of a Youth, Lessons from My Father.* He is married to Margaret and they are blessed with children.

Lightning Source UK Ltd.
Milton Keynes UK
UKOW05f0931180417
299339UK00001B/14/P